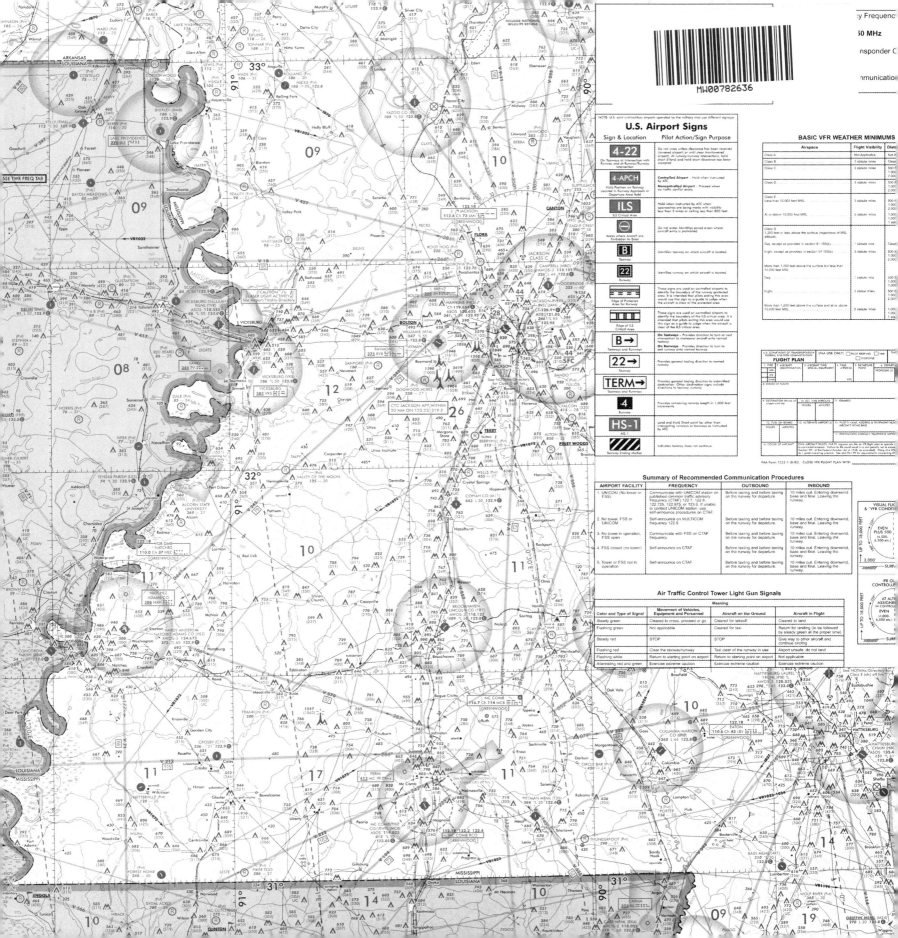

LOUISIANA AVIATION

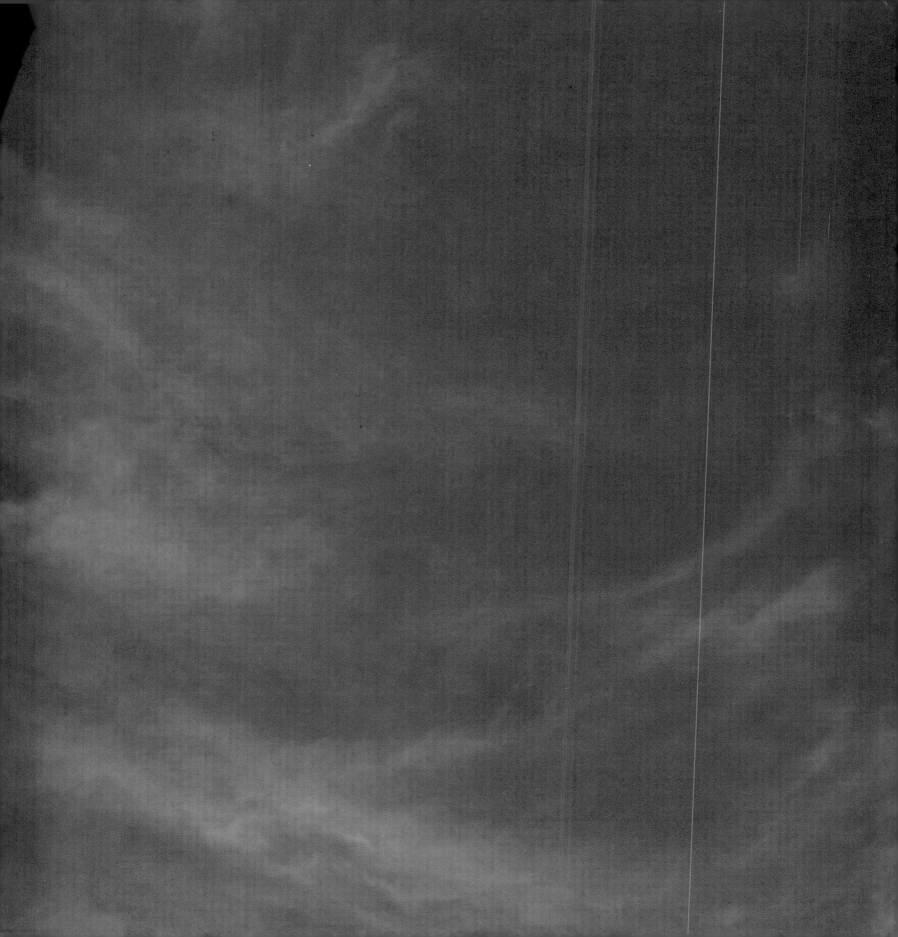

Caldwell Parish Library
Louisiana aviation : an extraordinary history in ...
Caire, Vincent, 1902-
0075   6704

DISCARD

VINCENT P. CAIRE

LOUISIANA AVIATION

AN EXTRAORDINARY HISTORY IN PHOTOGRAPHS

LOUISIANA STATE UNIVERSITY PRESS

BATON ROUGE

Published by Louisiana State University Press
Copyright © 2012 by Louisiana State University Press
All rights reserved
Manufactured in China
First printing

DESIGNER: Barbara Neely Bourgoyne
TYPEFACE: Whitman
PRINTER AND BINDER: C&C Offset

LIBRARY OF CONGRESS CATALOGING-IN-PUBLICATION DATA
Caire, Vincent, 1962–
  Louisiana aviation : an extraordinary history in photographs / Vincent Caire.
      p. cm.
  Includes bibliographical references and index.
  ISBN 978-0-8071-4210-3 (cloth : alk. paper) — ISBN 978-0-8071-4211-0 (pdf :
alk. paper) — ISBN 978-0-8071-4212-7 (epub : alk. paper) — ISBN 978-0-8071-
4213-4 (mobi : alk. paper) 1. Aeronautics—Louisiana—History. 2. Aeronautics—
Louisiana—History—Pictorial works. I. Title.
  TL726.3.L8C35 2012
  387.709763—dc23

                                                              2011020452

The paper in this book meets the guidelines for permanence and durability
of the Committee on Production Guidelines for Book Longevity of the Council
on Library Resources. ∞

Caldwell Parish Library
P.O. Box 1499
Columbia, La. 71418

For

Rachel, Robyn, Paul, and Cindy

Mom and Dad

Steve, Betsy, Roddy, Mag, Tez, and Elia

Thanks for keeping my head in and out of the clouds

CONTENTS

Right, Throughout the 1970s and 1980s, Corkey Fornof of Houma, Louisiana, performed the aerial stunts in the James Bond 007 films.

Below left, Corkey has appeared in numerous commercials aired throughout the world, including this flight through a hangar for Toshiba filmed in the late 1970s.

Below right, In the 1960s and early 1970s, Corkey and his father, the late Korean War ace J. W. "Bill" Fornof, one of the United States Navy's most decorated aviators, performed together in a pair of Grumman Bearcats for air shows throughout the country. (Photos courtesy of Corkey Fornof)

FOREWORD

When Vince told me he was going to write a book about Louisiana aviation, the first thing that came to mind was, What took you so long? What a great subject! I have been flying since I was a teenager, beginning over south Louisiana, and now all over the world for the motion picture and TV industry. Some of the most exciting aerial scenes I developed for the James Bond films were inspired by my Louisiana experiences. For instance, the seaplane sequence in 007's *License to Kill* comes from my early flying adventures above and along our bayous. I have filmed many other major motion pictures and TV commercials here. Yes, I am a Louisiana boy through and through!

Wherever I fly, I am often asked about our Louisiana aviation pioneers. From Patterson's one-of-a-kind Wedell-Williams aircraft that dominated the "Golden Age of Air Racing" in the 1930s to the founding of Delta Air Lines out of an innovative crop-dusting operation in Tallulah and Monroe, our legends span the state. This book tells their story.

I love to fly! And when I taxi my aircraft to the active runway for takeoff, I love the look in the eyes of the youngsters, and the youngsters at heart, who honor us all by coming to see our performances at air shows. And here's a little secret. To tell you the truth, I have as much fun speaking with armchair pilots as I do with my professional associates. I am energized by that passion to be a part of aviation. Louisiana is still home to some great pilots—just ask a few, and they'll be happy to tell you how great they are!

I have no doubt that once you begin to glance through these stories and photographs, you will want to know more about Louisiana aviation, from the earliest flights, through the war years and heroes, to the aircraft and people that built and support major industries— and then, of course, there are guys like me, the privileged who get to fly for the movies, Louisiana style! Welcome to the world of flying! You will certainly enjoy the ride. I'm looking forward to seeing you at the next air show. And remember to check your six o'clock position!

I love and thank you, Louisiana.

J. W. "Corkey" Fornof

Shushan Airport, south shore of Lake Pontchartrain, New Orleans, 1934.
(Photo courtesy of the Shushan Collection, Earl K. Long Library, University
of New Orleans)

A NOTE ABOUT LOUISIANA AVIATION

Aviation truly touches every part of our lives, and the benefits it brings to our community border on being immeasurable. For example, agricultural crop spraying, or "crop-dusting," ensures healthy food for our tables. General civil aviation supports, among other activities, firefighting and the medical and emergency services that keep our families and properties safe. Of the thousands of aircraft arriving and departing through Louisiana's network of airport facilities, commercial airliners account for only a small percentage.

In addition to their recreational flying, hundreds of volunteer pilots donate their time and aircraft each month to transport patients from our smallest community runways to renowned health facilities so that our neighbors may receive the best specialized care possible. Small business and corporate aircraft transport local executives around the globe with the goal of bringing economic development back home to our communities. Helicopter and seaplane operations supporting the petrochemical industry are a common sight across Louisiana.

In fact, aviation's overall economic impact in our state is well over $3 billion annually, and the derived intangible benefit to the state is greater still. There are more than 780 landing facilities throughout Louisiana, including public-use airports, private-use airports, heliports, seaplane bases, and agricultural landing facilities.

This book captures the historical heart and passion of the development of aviation in Louisiana. It complements one of the missions of the Louisiana Department of Transportation and Development–Aviation Division, which is to help our residents better understand Louisiana's aviation infrastructure. Our objective is to continue building on an already safe, modern, and well-managed aviation system to provide convenient and efficient access throughout our state, from the largest to the smallest communities.

I know that you will find this work informative, and I hope it will encourage your interest in aviation in your parish and local community. There is plenty to see and do out there!

Here's to happy flying in Louisiana, past, present, and future!

Brad Brandt, Director of Aviation,
Louisiana Department of Transportation and Development

LOUISIANA AVIATION

A morning sky over Lake Pontchartrain framed within the contrails of jet aircraft on transcontinental flights miles above Louisiana. (Photo by the author)

INTRODUCTION

Louisiana skies play a significant role in U.S. civil aviation. This collection of historic and contemporary photographs introduces the places and personalities associated with this little-known legacy. Spanning the Pelican State—from the banks of the Red River in Shreveport and Alexandria, the cotton fields of Monroe, and down to the bayou country of Houma, Patterson, Lake Charles, and Lafayette—these images offer a unique aerial journey through civilian aviation in Louisiana. Introduced here are the Louisiana personalities that made air travel an industry, inspiring and paving the way for today's commercial and business aviation infrastructure that so heavily influences the lives and economies of our generation.

Today, Louisiana is home to an incredible variety of aviation facilities dedicated to many specializations ranging from agricultural applications to petrochemical support and commercial airline travel. Several are capable of supporting the most complex global industry operations. In addition to its historic nature, this book also introduces what Louisiana offers the contemporary aviation community, giving Louisiana residents a heightened awareness of the economic value of these facilities statewide.

Military aviation has played an integral role in the development of our state's airports, and the influence of wartime operations is discussed in this narrative. However, the rich history of military aviation in Louisiana demands dedicated coverage all to itself, and a comprehensive narrative of such heroism will follow in a later companion publication.

The objective of this volume is twofold. The first is to introduce the influential Louisiana citizens who have had an impact on American aviation. The second is to highlight some of the facilities that paved the way for aviation along Louisiana's bayous, rivers, and farmlands. In an effort to most effectively introduce this important Louisiana story, this collection is presented in nontechnical terms and welcomes readers with little or no background in aviation. However, it will also pique the interest of those already acquainted with the subject matter.

Contemporary Louisiana aviation is supported by a captivating sense of community. Promising young professionals desiring a future in the skies have access to a remarkable range of statewide resources. Intrastate aviation, like other industries, navigates through an endless series of peaks and troughs with variances in revenue that affect local economic bases. Louisiana's aviation infrastructure is no exception. When fully functioning statewide aviation resources are present, supporting transportation for the businesses, industries, and personal pleasures of Louisiana communities, it inevitably attracts other businesses capable of creating jobs and increasing revenues, establishing firm support for our economy. Please sit back, relax, and enjoy the flight.

CHAPTER ONE

BEGINNINGS

The sky presents humanity with a tempting challenge. Though curious and ever versatile, human beings are simply incapable of naturally defying gravity or maneuvering above the surface of the earth.

For thousands of years prior to the aeronautical revolutions in the twentieth century, flight was a dream, spawning a homo sapien envy of winged creatures who moved freely through the air, a sensation humans could experience only in fiction. On December 17, 1903, the Wright Brothers broke earth's terrestrial grasp, forever changing the course of human and technological evolution. The first human flight, lasting little more than twelve seconds and boasting an altitude of fewer than twenty feet, gave birth to the possibility. Seven years later, Louisiana residents witnessed this breakthrough for the first time.

Made up of waterways and few unchallenging land routes, Louisiana would seem to be an appropriate setting in which to introduce the airplane. Residents were constantly challenged in crossing rivers, bayous and basins, adjacent swampland, and other, less passable terrain. However, the state's residents initially showed little interest in embracing aviation's possibilities. Those who believed in the future of flying would need to convince skeptical audiences still attached to nineteenth-century travel habits.

Much of this cold reception can be attributed to the circus-like introduction of aviation. Early demonstrations appeared to showcase a novelty, not a necessity. Suspending human beings in the air at the mercy of a machine, though an intriguing idea, seemed a frivolous pursuit in a state whose economy was overwhelmingly dependent on agriculture, trapping, and limited manufacturing. And Louisiana was not alone in its less than enthusiastic response to aviation; communities throughout the United States were slow to embrace the idea of flight as a useful instrument of daily routine.

John Bevins Moisant, from Kankakee, Illinois, along with brother Alfred and sister Matilde, abandoned care of family business interests and dedicated themselves to the possibilities of the airplane. With a knack for showmanship, the trio established one of the first successful public air demonstrations in the era between the Wright Brothers' 1903 flight and the start of World War I in 1914.

The wealthy trio supported themselves in part through a plantation operation in El Salvador and other interests in Central America. John Moisant earned his wings in France and was one of the first pilots to fly across the English Channel. His fame in the United States began when New York newspapers covered his victory in an aircraft race whose course included circling the Statue of Liberty. John Moisant embarked on a tour of North America and was soon joined by Alfred, who managed the finances, while Matilde served as promoter, preparing each city in advance for demonstration flights and then often thrilled crowds by flying herself.

"The Moisant Flyers" traveled throughout the United States, winning celebrity status wherever they went. In the last week of December 1910, the Flyers traveled to New Orleans to support John in his attempt to capture a standing cash prize, known as the Michelin Cup, awarded to the person who could stay aloft in an airplane for the longest period that year.

One of the first aircraft flights over New Orleans occurred on February 6, 1910. (Courtesy of The Historic New Orleans Collection)

Moisant performed his flight on December 31, 1910, to ensure that no other flyer would have time to surpass his duration in the air. Civic leaders welcomed the trio and their entourage with pageantry worthy of a royal family. Moisant took off from City Park, navigated along the Mississippi River to an area of open farmland approximately seven miles west of New Orleans along the east bank of the river, where he would fly over the waiting crowd to accomplish his record-setting feat.

While maneuvering slowly at low altitude, a gust of wind overtook his aircraft and pushed him into the ground. Moisant was thrown out of the cockpit, receiving a fatal neck injury. He died while being transported by train to a hospital in New Orleans. Alfred and Matilde accepted an invitation for him to be buried in Metairie Cemetery. Years later his remains were relocated to a family plot in North Hollywood, California. In light of such introductions, human flight was slow to move out of the realm of novelty. Gradually, however, forward-thinking citizens began to consider the possibilities of aviation.

PIONEERING AIRMAIL SERVICE

Adventurous pilots who flew in the skies over Europe in World War I returned to the United States in late 1918 without an aviator's mission. Although military aviation began over the battlefields of the Great

Top left, John Bevins Moisant and his brother Alfred discussing his flight demonstration with curious onlookers on December 31, 1910.

Top right, John Bevins Moisant flying over Harahan moments before his fatal crash on December 31, 1910. Spectators on the ground are using white cloths to mark the landing area for the inbound flyer.

Left, John Moisant's aircraft after the crash on December 31, 1910. (Photos courtesy of Miles McCormick)

Top, George Mestache and onlookers in front of his aircraft on April 10, 1912, the day of his first airmail flight from New Orleans City Park to the original LSU Campus in Baton Rouge.

Bottom, George Mestache receives his 32-pound sack of mail bound for Baton Rouge on April 10, 1912. The bag held a special letter delivered to Governor Jared Y. Sanders Sr. (Photos courtesy of The Historic New Orleans Collection)

War, the civilian home front of 1918 had, at best, limited use for the skills of a battle-born flyer. Purchasing surplus military aircraft, veterans sought any work put before them, traveling from one end of the nation to the other seeking a means of supporting themselves. Affectionately known as "barnstormers," they attracted paying audiences by selfishly presenting flying to the public as a daring and dangerous profession. They perpetuated this image with the spectacles they staged in farm fields, public parks, and horse racing tracks. Citizens accepted the airplane as a military instrument but did not imagine it as having commercial use, much less as a practical means of transporting human beings across vast distances.

One group of such pilots attempting to make a living in New Orleans set up shop downriver in Belle Chasse, christening their field in honor of Alvin Callender, a fellow flyer killed in Europe. Their promise of speed attracted bankers, and the operation supported itself by transporting checks between major cities. Upon realizing that managers in financial industries were impressed, these early aviators made a point to transport checks, bonds, and other valued documents faster than the railroads.

Confidence in aircraft steadily increased. The U.S. Postal Service believed this new means of swift transport would enhance delivery. The era of airmail began in 1923, when local postmasters offered loosely enforced contracts to carry mail relatively short distances that were obviously impractical and challenging by land, such as over waterways and rugged terrain. Route systems were developed near key population centers. The operations were often unorganized, staffed by enthusiasts more interested in flying than in the actual business of airmail carriage. In the eyes of the public, however, it was this activity that legitimized the civilian flying of these former World War I pilots.

The Kelly Air Mail Act of 1925 officially established the authority of the U.S. postmaster to create airmail routes across state lines, approve standards, and execute federal airmail contracts, or Contract Air Mail (CAM) and Foreign Air Mail (FAM) routes.

Local postmasters continued to authorize the routes deemed most beneficial to the communities. But following this success, extensive networks were developed and awarded by national bid. The mail was collected in the city, often brought in from other communities via rail, staged by the local post office, and then, in the case of the Alvin Callender operation, transported via ferry across the river to the airmail carriers.

A marker identifies the spot near the State Capitol Building where Mestache landed in Baton Rouge. (Photo by the author)

Photographs of airmail pilots and ground crews such as this one taken in the mid-1920s were often staged promotional affairs rather than efforts to document the operation itself. Note the gentleman wearing the mechanic's overalls over his business suit. (Photo courtesy of the Jon Proctor Collection)

Left, A De Havilland airmail biplane in flight in 1927 between destinations.

Bottom left, Pilots and crews prepare for an evening airmail flight sometime in the late 1920s. (Photos courtesy of the Jon Proctor Collection)

MERRILL RIDDICK

For some time after the end of World War I, veteran pilots remained an eccentric collection of daredevils, frequently finding it difficult to relinquish their passion for the air and adjust to the more moderate pace of civilian life. In 1923, Merrill Riddick, a member of this elite corps of flyers, was pleased to learn that the U.S. Postal Service had accepted his bid submitted earlier that year to execute Foreign Air Mail Route 3 (FAM–3), a contract to transport mail via floatplane between New Orleans and Pilot Town.

The postmaster wanted to expedite delivery of mail to ships that had left the city docks days earlier and were preparing to exit the mouth of the river destined for foreign ports. The contract also required accepting mail from inbound vessels anchored at Pilot Town awaiting their turn to enter the port of New Orleans. Unsure of just how he would carry out this mission, Riddick borrowed two thousand dollars from his father to purchase an Aeromarine floatplane and establish Gulf Coast Air Lines, Inc.

Riddick mastered and refined the procedures for a tricky routine. Taking off from the banks of the Mississippi at the foot of Carrollton Avenue, he followed the twists of the river searching for specific vessels, circling, then landing nearby and maneuvering the seaplane alongside the ship, all the while fighting a strong river current and surface winds. With sacks of mail exchanged and following a brief check of his engine, he was then often forced to maneuver out of the paths of other vessels for takeoff on the water. Upon return to New Orleans, Riddick anchored his aircraft on the bank and reported to the postmaster's office to deliver the inbound post and receive his due earnings of forty dollars per round-trip.

The local postmaster often withheld payment for unspecified reasons, frustrating an already agitated pilot whose energies were expended fighting natural and mechanical elements in getting the job done. It is entirely possible that the postmaster simply did not care for Riddick's one-man method of accomplishing the task. Finally, after only eleven trips down the river and back, Riddick abandoned his contract in frustration. He left the New Orleans area, eventually settling in the Midwest to join other airmail pilots on established airmail routes.

The New Orleans to Pilot Town route, spanning a mere eighty miles in flight, was one of the first airmail contracts established by the U.S. Postal Service that required use of amphibious aircraft. Others included service linking Key West, Florida, to Havana, Cuba; and Seattle, Washington, to Victoria, British Columbia, Canada. Riddick's FAM–3 route was unique in that it was the only Foreign Air Mail contract that did not require the pilot to fly the aircraft into a foreign nation. Sometime after Riddick's departure, the contract was modified and reassigned to a new service provider, New Orleans Air Line, founded specifically for the task. The new operation incorporated multiple aircraft and pilots, thus affording the postmaster greater reliability. Credit for its success, however must be given to Riddick, who pioneered the procedure and route as a one-man operation.

Merrill Riddick accepts U.S. mail bound for Honduras that he will deliver aboard his aircraft to a ship already under way out of New Orleans (1923). (Photo courtesy of the Historic New Orleans Collection)

One of the most influential events in the progress of aviation was Charles Lindbergh's flight across the Atlantic Ocean in May 1927. The distance between Europe and North America shrank when Lindbergh's *Spirit of St. Louis* Ryan monoplane arrived from New York's Roosevelt Field at Paris, France's Le Bourget Airport. Followed by every newspaper and radio station on earth, his success was a global achievement, repositioning human flight from possibility to reality. Known as the "Lone Eagle" and "Lucky Lindy," Lindbergh had just the right combination of determination and charisma to make the trip across the Atlantic and attract the attention of entrepreneurs who could finance the growth and development of aviation.

The philanthropist Daniel Guggenheim was so impressed with Lindbergh's achievement that, upon the hero's return from France, he financed a tour of the United States for the aviator so that as many people as possible could see the flyer and his aircraft in person. Named the Guggenheim Tour for its financier, the journey was meant to "encourage interest and research in aviation." The three-month event sponsored Lindbergh's personal visit to all forty-eight states, including stops in ninety-two cities along the route, beginning at Mitchell Airport, Long Island, on July 20, 1927, and officially ending at the same location three months later, on October 23, 1927.

Lindbergh selected New Orleans as Louisiana's tour stop. Although farmlands and surrounding areas on the east bank of the Mississippi River had been used irregularly as landing sites, Alvin Callender Airfield in nearby Belle Chasse was the only landing field officially endorsed by the City of New Orleans.

Lindbergh flew into New Orleans on October 8, 1927, arriving from his previous stop in Jackson, Mississippi, following a flyover of Franklinton, Louisiana. He circled the downtown New Orleans area and proceeded to find Alvin Callender. At that time, there were no local radio navigation signals to support his flights, requiring him to follow the river for the short journey to the Belle Chasse airstrip.

The visit generated countless newspaper articles and event-related advertisements throughout the state. Upon landing, Lindbergh greeted the mayor and his entourage, who promptly transported him by boat to downtown New Orleans. Civic leaders, including those of smaller Louisiana cities attending Lindbergh's historic visit, instantly recognized the potential and importance of aviation. Upon their return home, each encouraged the growth of airmail in their area.

In October 1927, this banner, handmade by an unknown Lindbergh admirer, was waved during Lindbergh's welcoming parade in New Orleans. (Artifact courtesy of the Louisiana State Museum; photo by the author)

Lindbergh's remarks were eye-opening, centering on the practical use of the airplane as a tool of business. In one of his most memorable comments, he expressed amazement that a city as large and important as New Orleans did not have an airport on the same side of the river as the majority of its population. He thought it ridiculous that the airport was located as an afterthought, miles down and across the Mississippi.

The Guggenheim Tour resulted in immediate interest in aviation by the general public and civic leaders, who now insisted on following Lindbergh's suggestion that plans be developed for an airport on the east bank of the river. The use of airmail was increasing exponentially nationwide.

Designed and Manufactured by Coleman E. Adler, New Orleans.

The following day, October 9, Lindbergh flew from Callender Airfield to the Pensacola Naval Air Station before continuing to Tallahassee and Jacksonville, Florida. During the tour, it was not uncommon for Lindbergh to alter his itinerary. He often took detours to overfly cities that were not planned stops, but which were, according to Guggenheim, "exploration tours that were interesting to Lindbergh himself."

This gift, designed by Coleman E. Adler as an aerial view of the city, was presented to Charles Lindbergh by the "Citizens of New Orleans" in celebration of his October 1927 visit. Note the lack of any airfields in the design. (Photo courtesy of the Louisiana State Museum)

ALVIN CALLENDER AIRFIELD, BELLE CHASSE, LOUISIANA

In 1918, a yellow fever epidemic overwhelmed the Gulf Coast. The City of New Orleans maintained a large military port infrastructure for transporting infantrymen, known as "doughboys," to and from the Great War in Europe. Rapid spread of the disease caused by the increased population and abundant mosquitoes moved many local landowners to drain swampland properties in an attempt to curb the infestation. George Hero Sr. followed suit on a small patch of riverfront land near his sugarcane plantation in Belle Chasse.

He allowed the grounds to be used as the city's first airfield, agreeing to the name Alvin Callender in honor of this local veteran hero killed in action. A small group of aviation enthusiasts maintained the field, operating surplus Army airplanes to cities along the Gulf Coast and as far away as Atlanta.

The field was active until 1928, the year following Charles Lindbergh's suggestion that a more practical location be found for a New Orleans airport. Alvin Callender Airfield remained open, offering pilots a small hangar maintained by the City of New Orleans. During World War II, it was used by the U.S. Navy as a remote field to support cadet pilot training out of the recently constructed Naval Air Station in New Orleans on the shore of Lake Pontchartrain. During the war, an extended concrete runway was built to support the military operations. For approximately thirty days in 1947, following a hurricane that flooded Moisant Field in Kenner, Callender served as the city's primary commercial airport for airline passengers.

In 1951, as the Cold War progressed, the City of New Orleans negotiated a transfer of Alvin Callender Airfield to the U.S. Navy for construction of an expanded Joint Reserve Base to replace the outgrown NAS New Orleans (now occupied by the University of New Orleans), a project spearheaded by Louisiana senators Russell Long and Allen Ellender. The Hero family, who still owned property surrounding the airfield, unsuccessfully filed a federal lawsuit to prevent the development, arguing that their father's intention had been to operate a much smaller municipal airport.

Today it is known simply as Naval Air Station New Orleans; the Alvin Callender name is now infrequently used. The base serves as a critical unit in the defense of the entire Gulf Coast, supporting fighter and patrol air units in reserve and active wings in the United States Navy, Air Force, Army, Marines, Coast Guard, and National Guard.

Alvin Callender Airfield, the site of Lindbergh's 1927 visit, pictured here in 2010, is now Naval Air Station New Orleans, a Joint Reserve air base supporting air operations for all military branches. (Photo by the author)

CHAPTER TWO

AN ERA OF ENTREPRENEURS

Between 1927 and 1935, flying advanced to center stage in popular culture, rivaling Hollywood in entertaining citizens throughout the country. Ironically, on its way to becoming one of the forces most influential in shaping the twentieth century, aviation shared the spotlight with the Great Depression. The unique sight of an aircraft in the air provided a welcome diversion from economic woes.

When the first air carriers began operating, passengers were a secondary source of revenue. Airmail and other utilities were the priority on scheduled flights that connected urban and remote locations. Support of agriculture played no small part in this evolution. As a result, Louisiana's rural and metropolitan communities offered fertile ground for the early stages of the evolving industry.

Top, Jimmie Wedell landing his aircraft at the brothers' first primitive airstrip near today's Canal Boulevard (1927). (Photo courtesy of the Louisiana State Museum)

Bottom, Air shows at Menefee Field, such as this one in 1929, offered opportunity for local promotions, one of which incorporated a bathing-suit contest and an air demonstration by this visiting Transcontinental Air Transport (TAT) mail plane. (Photo courtesy of the Newman Collection, Earl K. Long Library, University of New Orleans)

Opposite, Walter Wedell prepares to "wing walk" with brother Jimmie at the controls at Menefee Field (1928). (Photo in author's collection)

GRASS STRIPS AND MUDDY LANDINGS

Entrepreneurial interest in aviation evolved from naïve curiosity into a world of possibility. Suddenly, makeshift airstrips on unsown farmland and open areas along frequented roadways were inadequate. Barnstormers who once settled anywhere there was available space began shedding their reputation as aerial clowns. Following Lindbergh's tour, flying was no longer simply an amusing sight, but rather an innovation destined to have an economic impact.

While Louisiana's introduction to aviation was similar to that in other parts of the country, one unique geographic trait—south Louisiana swampland—provided a major incentive for local development. Narrow navigation channels inherited from prior generations were inadequate for contemporary transportation. Flying bypassed these challenging routes.

While barnstormers often looked no further into the future than the next performance, a new breed of enthusiasts appeared who recognized aviation as a business. In communities across Louisiana, nomadic flyers began to use airfields rather than open farmland, establishing home bases at permanent locations. Operations were modest in scope, often little more than circular-shaped acreage with a single dilapidated barn serving as a hangar to shelter the aircraft.

Curious patrons paid entrance fees to view private airfield exhibitions and see an airplane up close. Those who dared could hire a plane and pilot to travel from one field to another in an open cockpit.

Aircraft operators eagerly searched for ways to support the operation. Most continued to bid on the highly competitive airmail routes as demand increased and local postmasters expanded networks to serve the state's larger communities of Baton Rouge, New Orleans, Shreveport, and Monroe. Few operators were awarded these contracts, and fewer still were able to depend on them as a regular source of revenue.

An undeveloped area near Canal Boulevard in New Orleans hosted one such budding operation. Brothers James "Jimmie" and Walter Wedell, natives of Texas, arrived in the city at the height of Lindbergh mania. Like other barnstormers, they were searching for an operating field, with the hope that the property owner would be supportive once introduced to the prospects of their flying operation.

The brothers were raised by their father, a widower who owned a bar in Texas City catering to Gulf Coast sailors and oil laborers. Jimmie Wedell barely survived a teenage motorcycle accident that resulted in blindness in one eye and a later rejection by the U.S. Army

Air Corps for pilot training. Undeterred, he purchased and repaired a pair of abandoned training aircraft. Although receiving random lessons from sympathetic pilots (who were happy to receive whiskey "borrowed" from their father's saloon as a token of appreciation), the Wedell brothers were self-taught pilots. Ironically, Jimmie Wedell was later briefly employed as a contracted civilian flight instructor at Kelly Army Airfield near San Antonio, Texas.

Soon thereafter, in the early days of Prohibition, the Wedell brothers became involved in the lucrative transportation of bootleg alcohol and firearms between Mexico and Texas. After approximately a year

of midnight operations, the pair relocated to New Orleans to start a legitimate flying business.

The Wedell brothers promoted their trade by flying low over the city, waving to people on the ground. The inquisitive onlookers followed the planes, would ask questions, and often, one of the brothers would take them up for a demonstration flight. There was no hangar on the site.

James Menefee, owner of a Chevrolet dealership on Canal Street and perhaps unaware of their recent international operations, was impressed by the pair's tenacity and determination. Menefee understood the impact of Lindbergh's visit to the city, and asked the brothers to manage an airport he wanted to open on property in Jefferson Parish. Menefee believed the operating cost would be offset by capitalizing on the city's lack of a proper airfield on the east bank of the Mississippi River. With a business plan and partnership founded, Menefee Airport opened to the public on Jefferson Highway on Sunday, June 24, 1928, attracting 7,500 spectators.

Pilots from other parts of the country used the Menefee Airport while passing through the city. Flying a new Ryan aircraft purchased by Menefee that was nearly identical to the aircraft Lindbergh had piloted to Paris, the Wedell brothers became local celebrities, participating in creative flyovers above south Louisiana. In one famous instance, Walter Wedell married his bride, Henrietta, on board the aircraft in flight as brother Jimmie piloted over downtown New Orleans. WWL radio covered the wedding ceremony from the airplane.

Operations throughout the state had similar beginnings. It is important to understand that airfields such as Menefee were private endeavors. Publicly owned municipal airports followed later. Although the Kelly Air Mail Act had begun to establish a network of mail routes, and the Department of Commerce followed suit, introducing the Air Commerce Act in 1926, setting minimum standards for pilot training, the construction of the nation's first airports was undertaken almost entirely by private citizens.

These early airfields did not have outlined runways. Pilots flew over the field, determined wind direction with the help of a windsock, and then landed. Prevailing wind patterns change little over time. As a result, the earliest runways evolved much like heavily traveled dirt roads, with the tire tracks laying the foundation through continuous use.

The operation prospered for one year under the watchful eyes of the Wedell brothers. Having gained practical business experience, however, they were no longer satisfied with piloting Menefee's customers, and James Wedell's desire to design his own airplanes began diverting his attention. By the time the brothers left the company in the summer of 1929, they were building an aircraft in a garage off the airport property.

James Menefee continued to operate the airport on his own, leasing the hangar to a steadily increasing number of aircraft owners in the city. He relocated to a field in St. Bernard Parish, directly across from the Chalmette Battlefield. The move proved a lucrative one. C. R. Smith, president of American Airways, contracted with Menefee to operate his New Orleans to Chicago passenger and airmail flights from the Chalmette airport. The "new" Menefee Airport was for a time referred to as "American Airways Field." For the next three years, until the construction of New Orleans Shushan Airport on Lake Pontchartrain, the airline's Ford and Fokker Tri-motor aircraft provided south Louisiana's first scheduled airline service from Menefee's dirt landing strip.

Menefee Airport in Chalmette remained active through World War II, providing military aviation cadets from the New Orleans Naval Air Station with, in addition to Alvin Callendar, a secondary outlying practice airfield for flight training. Over time, the property changed hands and was divided and developed into commercial and residential lots. A single original hangar used by Menefee and American Airways clings to life on the property. Though modified by a number of occupants, its origins as an aircraft hangar are obvious to the keen observer.

Menefee Field, 1928. Standard Oil provided the majority of Louisiana airfields with aviation gasoline. (Photo courtesy of the Newman Collection, Earl K. Long Library, University of New Orleans)

Top left, In 1929, Menefee Air Service became a dealer for Swallow Aircraft, a manufacturer preceding today's Cessna, Piper, and Beechcraft companies. Jimmie and Walter Wedell were the sales representatives. (Photo courtesy of the Newman Collection, Earl K. Long Library, University of New Orleans)

Top right, By the early 1930s and much like Menefee Field in New Orleans, communities such as Mansfield began constructing primitive sod airfields in the hope of luring airmail service. (Photo courtesy of the Louisiana State Library)

Above, When American Airways inaugurated service from Menefee Airport to Jackson, Mississippi, and Chicago, the field was informally renamed American Airways Field. Interestingly, as this photograph taken in Jackson shows, one of the VIP passengers on board was Abe Shushan, who was in the throes of constructing an airport for the Orleans Levee District on Lake Pontchartrain. (Photo courtesy of the Abe Shushan Collection, Earl K. Long Library, University of New Orleans)

JAMES MENEFEE

James Menefee (*right*) assists Jimmie Wedell (*far left*) in preparing a Menefee Flying Service aircraft for a demonstration (1929). (Photo courtesy of the Louisiana State Museum)

Fascinated with automobiles, mechanics, and horsepower in the early twentieth century, New Orleans entrepreneur James Menefee established one of the first car dealerships in the city, opening his Chevrolet showroom at 1500 Canal Street. His interest in speed naturally drew him toward aviation.

Menefee was, by all accounts, a conservative businessman who appreciated the talents of the Wedell brothers but harbored no desire to risk financing their experiments and dreams of building airplanes. Following James and Walter's departure from the company, the Menefee/Wedell relationship remained cordial, and Menefee continued to offer the brothers use of his airfield for the planes they began building.

THE WEDELL-WILLIAMS AIR SERVICE IN PATTERSON, LOUISIANA

The city of Patterson in St. Mary Parish, Louisiana, is approximately eighty miles southwest of New Orleans. Although located in what would seem one of the most unlikely regions for pilots to congregate and prosper in their trade, the aerial activity in this area from 1929 through 1936 rightfully resulted in it being christened "The Birthplace of Speed Aviation in the United States."

Harry Palmerston Williams's upbringing in Patterson, Louisiana, sharply contrasts with that of the Wedell brothers in Texas City. Williams was a silver-spooned philanthropist and former mayor of his hometown, with a passion for fast automobiles. Financial fortune allowed him to indulge his lifelong thirst for adventure. Harry was born on October 6, 1889, the son of the Louisiana cypress lumber magnate Frank B. Williams; he and his siblings inherited the fortune his father had created from harvesting the vast resources of the south Louisiana cypress swampland. Following service in World War I, Harry took his place in the family industry. Harry made headlines nationwide when he married the silent-screen actress Marguerite Clark, who gave up her career on the Hollywood silver screen to reside in Patterson with her husband.

Governor Huey Long, attracted to Williams's unlimited financial and social influence in the southern United States, asked him to chair both the state Department of Highways and the Department of Corrections. Feeling constrained in the positions, Williams soon resigned, though he and Long maintained a politically convenient friendship throughout their lives.

Harry Williams met Jimmie Wedell when the latter landed one of James Menefee's aircraft on a Patterson farm. The result was an instantaneous friendship and the sharing of a mutual passion for flying. Wedell promptly taught Williams how to fly and told him of his desire to build fast airplanes.

Within months the pair founded the Wedell-Williams Air Service, incorporated on May 11, 1929, and headquartered in the Whitney Bank Building on Camp Street in New Orleans. In three years, their combined assets of raw talent and abundant financial resources captured the attention of the entire aviation world. Senator Long relished the publicity Louisiana gained through the increasing exploits of the aviation team, especially those of Jimmie Wedell, who soon challenged James Doolittle as the fastest pilot in the country. Wedell's flights

Top, Jimmie Wedell (*right*) describes his aircraft designs to Harry Williams (*left*) with simple chalkboard drawings (1933). (Photo courtesy of the Louisiana State Museum)

Bottom, Williams cleared a family sugarcane field to establish his Patterson base of operations (1929). (Photo courtesy of the Newman Collection, Earl K. Long Library, University of New Orleans)

shared front-page headlines with baseball players, famous bootleggers, and the federal recovery program campaigns, along the way entertaining the nation's population as it wrestled with the Depression.

A private company airfield was constructed on a ninety-acre pasture beside the Mississippi River in Jefferson Parish, eight miles west of New Orleans. Williams selected the site because within a mile of the area, Governor Long intended to construct Louisiana's first trans–Mississippi River bridge (today's Huey P. Long Bridge) to connect the East and West Banks.

Offices were opened in Baton Rouge, Alexandria, and Shreveport. A northern route served Jackson, Mississippi; Memphis, Tennessee; and St. Louis, Missouri. Dallas and Fort Worth, Texas, were served from Shreveport. Williams purchased Lockheed Vega airliners, the most technologically advanced passenger aircraft available, seating seven and preceding the introduction of the famous Douglas DC-3 by five years. The air service carried passengers but, for a number of reasons, was unsuccessful in obtaining an airmail route between any cities served by the company.

Williams faced a political challenge unique among air service entrepreneurs of the day, an unfortunate by-product of his friendship with Senator Long. The U.S. postmaster, James Farley, who also served as chairman of the Democratic National Committee, sought financially sound companies for airmail contracts. The decisions of the postmaster, however, were not immune to the influences of Presi-

dent Roosevelt following his election in 1932. The Wedell-Williams Air Service possessed a financial backbone that rivaled other air service corporations of the time, leaving no question of its ability to provide reliable service to the postmaster and grow with forecasted demand. Roosevelt's concern over a potential political challenge, given Senator Long's increased visibility and the popularity of his "Share the Wealth" program, cannot be discounted as an explanation for the difficulties Williams faced in gaining access to early airmail contracts for the airline operation.

In March 1934, both Harry Williams and James Wedell testified before a congressional committee in Washington, D.C., expressing concern for the future well-being of smaller airlines such as the Wedell-Williams Air Service should they be unable to secure contracts and compete with larger airlines. Their persistence resulted in the company eventually being awarded authority to operate a single mail route between New Orleans and Houston following American Airlines' withdrawal of service from New Orleans.

Paralleling Harry Williams's work to expand the airline on routes throughout the South was James Wedell's construction of racing aircraft, which began immediately after the company was founded. Williams agreed to finance construction of air racing planes if Wedell designed a ship that could carry mail faster than any other aircraft of the day, thus offering a unique angle for competing for these lucrative contracts. Initially, Wedell built two airframes named after the newly

Air service operations were opened on Jefferson Highway outside of New Orleans after the Patterson field was established (1931).

Opposite left, The air service racers were assembled in the Patterson hangar (1932).

Opposite right, Students of the Patterson flight school established by the air service (1933). (Photos courtesy of the Newman Collection, Earl K. Long Library, University of New Orleans)

formed partnership. The first, christened *We-Will*, featured a special airmail compartment. Its near identical but smaller twin, the *We-Will, Jr.*, lacking the cargo compartment, was built specifically for national air racing competitions.

Between 1929 and 1934, record-setting races propelled the Wedell-Williams Air Service into the national headlines. Jimmie Wedell developed a series of aircraft that dominated the air racing circuits. Harry Williams had complete confidence in his partner, providing the financial resources to build record-setting competitors for closed-course pylon and transcontinental air racing, making the Patterson-based brand one of the most respected in the world.

Since the postal route between Shreveport and New Orleans had been awarded to American Airways, the *We-Will* airframe was modified and became Harry Williams's personal aircraft, christened the *92*. The *We-Will, Jr.*, piloted exclusively by Jimmie Wedell, was rechristened the *44*. The aircraft became the first to exceed 300 miles per hour in these competitions.

James Wedell's fame as a designer began in September 1931 through a series of appearances at competitions throughout the country, the most famous being the Bendix Air Race. The purpose of the competition was to recognize ingenuity in the pursuit of speed racing. The then unknown *44* finished in second place in competitions that year.

Impressed by the performance, the aerial celebrity Roscoe Turner asked Wedell if he would build an identical airplane to his specifica-

tions and have it ready for the 1932 Bendix and Thompson National Air Races. Wedell obliged, and like the existing Wedell-Williams airframes, Turner's new racer was designed for both events. Turner's relationship with the Patterson factory gave the company instant notoriety. In the 1932 Bendix competition, the three Wedell-Williams racers, *92*, *44*, and Turner's *121*, placed first, second, and third.

Since Harry Williams did not fly his aircraft in competitions, the *92* was flown by several contracted pilots, the most famous being the husband-and-wife partnership of James and Mary Hazlip. James Hazlip was an associate of James Doolittle, both employed by the Shell Oil Company, and Mary was a versatile pilot in her own right. The pair made history when Mary Hazlip flew the *92* to a 1932 women's speed record, which occurred prior to the ascension of Amelia Earhart in the later 1930s as the world's most famous female pilot.

In the 1932 Bendix race, Doolittle flew to victory, lapping all of the aircraft in the race with the exception of James Wedell's *44*, which placed second, followed by Turner's *121*, placing third, and James Hazlip in the *92*, placing fourth.

In 1933, the victories continued. Wedell piloted the *44* to first place in the Thompson National Trophy Race. Wedell was followed by the *92*, flown by contracted pilot William Gehlbach. Roscoe Turner finished third but was penalized for an infraction early in the race. The victories established the company's reputation as an innovative force with a practical monopoly on speed and endurance.

Below, From 1930 through 1936, Ray Braud, manager of the Wedell-Williams operation and airport in New Orleans, played a critical role in the company's daily flights. Braud became a close confidant of the Wedell brothers and Harry Williams. (Photo courtesy of Mrs. Beverly Braud Murphy)

Above, One of the original Wedell-Williams New Orleans Airport flight logs maintained by Ray Braud in 1933. The logbook is stored at the Louisiana State Museum in Patterson. (Artifact courtesy of the Louisiana State Museum; photo by the author)

Top right, Jimmie Wedell understood the value of promotion and sponsorship for the company. Here he is advertising Crosley Radio Equipment, one of the leading distributors of electronic gear for the aviation and broadcasting industries (1931). (Photo courtesy of the Newman Collection, Earl K. Long Library, University of New Orleans)

Jimmie Wedell's and Harry Williams's passion attracted pilots from around the country to the south Louisiana operation, some from other companies, and others from the 1920s barnstorming circuits. Many, specifically on the airline side, often stayed only briefly and then moved on to other flying jobs, their names lost to history.

The air racer pilots, however, were a different breed. Their quest to capture high-speed glory by flying these cutting-edge planes is reminiscent of the efforts of today's high-profile athletes, and many, such as Turner and Hazlip, became household names to fans of the 1930s Golden Age of Aviation. As families across the country tuned their radios to the national air races, these individuals made Wedell-Williams a staple of national entertainment in the early days of the Depression.

In February 1934, Wedell introduced his newest aircraft design, the Model 45, at the opening ceremony of New Orleans's Shushan Airport, which hosted the Pan American Mardi Gras Air Race, an ill-fated attempt to establish an annual competition in the city. The company was also building an aircraft designed for the world competition Melbourne, Australia, to London, England, Air Race later that year. Wedell was especially pleased with the aircraft, which was the product of a newly established partnership funded by Williams between the air service and the Delgado Trade School, School of Aviation.

In the face of such dynamic success, the career of James Wedell would end tragically in an aircraft accident on June 24, 1934, while he was flying a British training aircraft, a De Havilland Gypsy Moth biplane owned by Williams. Now an avid aircraft collector who seldom flew the planes he acquired, Williams had purchased the plane against the advice of Wedell. Williams eventually agreed to get rid of some of the collection, including the Gypsy Moth, to make more space for Wedell, who complained he no longer had room to work in the Patterson hangar. An interested buyer asked for a demonstration flight, insisting that James Wedell be at the controls. Immediately following takeoff, the aircraft climbed steeply, then stalled at a very low altitude, crashing just beyond the Patterson airport runway. The potential buyer, Frank Sneeringer of Mobile, Alabama, suffered a fractured skull, a broken knee, and a concussion. James Wedell died on impact. Harry Williams blamed himself for his partner's death because he was killed in an aircraft from his personal collection.

Williams asked veteran air racer Doug Davis to fly the 44 in the 1934 Bendix and Thompson Races in August and September respectively. Davis easily won the August Bendix competition. During the September Thompson race the following month, however, Davis turned the plane early, before passing the racing pylon. Realizing his error, Davis circled, returning to the correct course by sharply banking the 44 to regain his place. Under the pressure of the turn, the aircraft's wing collapsed. The aircraft fell to the ground, killing Davis. Roscoe Turner, who had been trailing close behind Davis in his Wedell-Williams 121 racer, finished in first place.

Following the deaths of his partner, James Wedell, and friend Doug Davis in rapid succession, Harry Williams developed an aversion for air racing. Although a great deal of time and money had been spent preparing the aircraft for the international London-Melbourne race, Williams now refused to allow any air service crew to fly in the contest. Walter Wedell pleaded with Williams for the chance to fly the race in honor of his late

brother. Senator Huey Long also asked Williams to keep the planned Wedell-Delgado partnership together for the race. The Louisiana legislature, then in session, passed a bill authorizing fifteen thousand dollars to fund the entry in honor of Jimmie Wedell. Late one night following an evening of heavy drinking, Williams stumbled into the hangar and destroyed the aircraft's wing with an axe, thus eliminating any possibility of the racing team's participation.

The following year, Walter Wedell died in a mysterious charter flight crash in the waters near the Chandeler Islands. At the crash site, the passenger's body was found in the pilot's seat, and a witness reported that the aircraft had been flying erratically. Investigators noted a suspicious injury on Walter's head that authorities believe may have occurred prior to ground impact. These findings have led some to conclude that Walter Wedell may have been the victim of one of the first hijackings in U.S. aviation history.

Williams was disgusted by the series of misfortunes. He had informal conversations with other aviation entrepreneurs about selling the company but did not follow through on any offers.

Tragedy struck its final blow to the company on the evening of May 19, 1936. Harry Williams and his chief pilot, James Worthen, died when Williams's personal business aircraft, a Beechcraft Staggerwing, crashed during takeoff at the Baton Rouge Airport. The loss of Williams and Worthen, the company's two remaining senior executives,

Williams opened a maintenance school and apprenticeship to keep up with his growing fleet of aircraft (1932). (Photo courtesy of the Newman Collection, Earl K. Long Library, University of New Orleans)

brought an end to any prospect of survival for the air service and airline. Williams's ashes were spread over the Patterson airfield and a portion was also laid to rest in his father's tomb at Metairie Cemetery in New Orleans.

Williams's widow, Marguerite Clark, having no interest in maintaining the operation and with no children to inherit the company, renegotiated with Eddie Rickenbacker, president of Eastern Airlines, who had previously approached Williams about buying the company. Raymond Braud, a senior Wedell-Williams manager responsible for the air service operation in New Orleans, was trusted by Clark to assess the company property for the sale to Rickenbacker.

Rickenbacker's interest centered on the airmail route from New Orleans to Houston and the company's fleet of Lockheed Vega passenger aircraft, a combined asset that would allow Eastern to enter the lucrative Texas airline market overnight.

The air service had another project tragically cut short just before Williams's death, the success of which might have transformed the economy of south Louisiana in the 1930s. Jimmie Wedell and Harry Williams had submitted the Model 45 design for consideration as a new generation fighter plane sought by the U.S. Army Air Corps. Wil-

liams was later authorized by the Corps to further develop the XP-34 pursuit aircraft prototype based on the Model 45. This interest on the part of the Air Corps recognized James Wedell's ingenuity as being on a level equal to that of designers at other larger national aircraft manufacturing companies. Unfortunately, the Corps became skeptical about the prospects for the project's success in the absence of Wedell, its original designer, and to Williams's dismay, the XP-34 project was canceled.

Legend surrounds the fate of the Wedell-Williams XP-34 specifications, with some historians suggesting that copies made their way to Japanese spies prior to World War II. Claims that Wedell's success with lightweight and long-range designs (a combination curiously elusive for more established U.S. aircraft manufacturers at the time) influenced the development of the Mitsubishi Zero—its prototype appearing one year later—are not entirely without merit. It is, in fact, difficult to dismiss the similarity of the lower fuselage, tail, and elevator design of the Model 45, on which the XP-34 was based, and that of the Mitsubishi Zero.

The achievements of the Wedell-Williams Air Service are not unlike those of Boeing, Lockheed, Douglas, Martin, and other pioneering aerospace corporations, each founded by strong personalities determined to transform aviation into a revolutionary American industry. Regrettably for Louisiana, its long-term stature in aviation was ended by the tragic deaths of Jimmie Wedell and Harry Williams.

Williams established passenger air service in the hope of obtaining coveted airmail contracts from the U.S. postmaster. Wedell-Williams provided service between south Louisiana and Shreveport, Houston, and Dallas with Lockheed Vega aircraft (1930). (Photo courtesy of the Newman Collection, Earl K. Long Library, University of New Orleans)

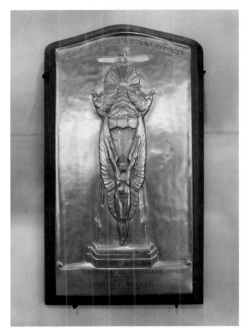

Top left, A Wedell-Williams airliner awaits passengers at the Patterson Airport (1930). (Photo courtesy of the Louisiana State Museum)

Top right, The air service offered unique charter flights to Grand Isle for executive fishing trips and private VIP getaways using amphibious aircraft (1932).

Left, In 1934, just months before his death, Jimmie Wedell, accompanied by Harry Williams, flew to Washington D.C. to testify before the House Subcommittee on Airmail Contracts. Williams stated publicly to the committee that the Wedell-Williams Air Service was being discriminated against in the award of lucrative routes.

Right, The 1933 first-place Thompson Trophy awarded to Jimmie Wedell for the transcontinental air race. The racing team's trophies are on display at the Wedell-Williams branch of the Louisiana State Museum in Patterson. (Photos by the author)

MARGUERITE CLARK

Orphaned while a young girl, Marguerite Clark was raised in New York City by her older sister following their parents' death. Her youthful beauty captured the attention of a motion picture industry in its infancy, and silent movie directors convinced her to pursue a career as an actress.

Clark's breakthrough role was her portrayal of Snow White in the original 1916 silent film version of the fairy tale. Her starring performance intrigued the then unknown midwestern cartoonist Walt Disney, influencing his 1939 interpretation of the story for his company's first full-length color cartoon. Clark was one of the most versatile of the earliest screen performers, and her popularity soared during World War I, with demand for her acting rivaling that of fellow starlets.

While participating in a bond drive, she was introduced to Army officer Harry P. Williams, whom she married at the end of the war. Clark surprised the industry by announcing she was abandoning her career and moving to Patterson to be with Williams. She starred in additional movies under the condition that filming was undertaken in her new home of south Louisiana. Eventually she gave up her career completely, relinquishing her earlier reign as the country's most popular young actress to her friend Mary Pickford.

When Harry Williams founded the Wedell-Williams Air Service, the couple had homes in Patterson, New York, and New Orleans, where Clark became a fixture of the city's social elite. She reigned as queen of several carnival balls, hosting parties at their St. Charles Avenue mansion (today the Latter Memorial Library). Their home in New York is said to have been Huey P. Long's getaway during his East Coast adventures. Clark recalled visits by Long, along with his demand that the shades be closed to prevent his assassination.

Clark was devastated by the successive deaths of the Wedell brothers in 1934 and 1935. The sudden loss of Harry Williams in 1936 left the

company solely in Clark's hands. She bowed to Eddie Rickenbacker's interest in the company, allowing him to name his own price if he would dispose of Harry's private aircraft collection as a personal favor.

By some accounts, Rickenbacker and other Eastern executives took advantage of Clark's desire to rid herself of the company. By others, he was Harry's friend, the one he would have most wanted to operate the airline. Clark sold the company to Eastern for approximately half its value after receiving assurance from Rickenbacker that the employees wanting to remain with the company would be allowed to do so. Many continued with Eastern Airlines in New Orleans or moved to other cities, grateful for the immediate job security during some of the harshest days of the Great Depression. Others departed, taking their talents elsewhere, having been too personally associated with Harry Williams and Jimmie and Walter Wedell to continue to work for the company under different leadership.

Relieved of Williams's companies and properties, Clark returned to New York to live with her sister, where she received adulation as a retired actress. Clark succumbed to pneumonia in 1940. She is buried in the Williams family tomb in Metairie Cemetery beside the ashes of her husband.

Above, After marrying Harry P. Williams, Marguerite Clark gave up a successful acting career. In 1916, she starred in the silent movie *Snow White,* inspiring Walt Disney's first production in animated feature films. (Photo courtesy of the New Orleans Public Library, Latter Memorial Branch)

Left, By 1933, Senator Huey P. Long (*right*) was smitten with the personality of Marguerite Clark (*left*). The senator and his wife were frequent guests at the Williamses' New York apartment. (Photo courtesy of the T. Harry Williams Papers, Mss. 2489, Louisiana and Lower Mississippi Valley Collections, Louisiana State University Libraries, Baton Rouge)

DELGADO TRADE SCHOOL, SCHOOL OF AVIATION

After founding the Wedell-Williams Air Service, Harry Williams and partner Jimmie Wedell understood that their mutual passion for building an aviation industry in Louisiana was dependent on a means to train eager individuals wishing to enter the profession as mechanics, pilots, and support personnel. In the first years of operating their new company, the pair befriended Byron Armstrong, a mechanic and fellow pilot.

Together the trio laid the groundwork for the Delgado Trade School, School of Aviation, opened in 1933 on the City Park campus. Williams provided significant political and financial support while Wedell and Armstrong introduced practical aircraft design ideas for the students to craft and assemble.

Though Jimmie Wedell designed his own racing planes at the Patterson Airport, this successful cooperative produced three unique aircraft constructed primarily by the Delgado Trade School that left a lasting impression on the sport of air racing in the 1930s—these were the *Delgado Maid,* the *Delgado Flash,* and the *Wedell-Williams MacRobertson Racer.*

The *Maid* (1933) and *Flash* (1937) were designed by Byron Armstrong to break global speed records. Unique in appearance and horsepower, the pair shared a common design of slender aerodynamic fuselages and short wingspans assembled under his tutelage by the Delgado Trade School students. Each was to be debuted in national air races.

Additional work on these aircraft was postponed when Jimmie Wedell entered the 1934 Mac Robertson Melbourne to London Race. Harry Williams enlisted the Delgado Trade School to support the assembly of the aircraft. The MacRobertson Racer was designed to provide the long-distance endurance necessary to complete the overwater global route. Like the *Maid* and the *Flash,* it was intended to attract public interest in the school and its mission of aviation education.

Jimmie Wedell's tragic death before the aircraft was completed crippled the program. After Harry Williams famously destroyed the aircraft in disgust, the Delgado Trade School students finished their second racer, the *Flash,* after his death in 1936. Although designed to be faster and more maneuverable than the original *Maid,* it never achieved the recognition of its counterpart.

The *Flash's* airframe was destroyed when the campus warehouse it was stored in caught on fire. Prior to crashing on a 1936 test flight,

Top, The *Delgado Maid* prior to a test flight at Shushan Airport in 1934.

Bottom, The *Delgado Flash* in the trade school hangar. In this photograph, believed to have been taken during testing in 1937, its propeller has been removed for maintenance. (Photos courtesy of the Louisiana State Museum)

the *Maid* was unofficially clocked at 375 miles per hour, making it the fastest land-based aircraft at that time.

The Delgado Trade School, School of Aviation remained open through the late 1980s. Students worked from a "hangar on campus" behind the original administration building. A second hangar located at the New Orleans Lakefront Airport served as the school's airfield training facility. State budget cuts eventually forced the program to close.

AIR RACING IN THE GOLDEN AGE OF AVIATION

Between 1929 and 1934, Jimmie Wedell designed and flew a series of aircraft that dominated national air racing winner's circles. He named many of the aircraft after calibers of firearms, christening his personal racer the *44*, and claiming it was "hot as a 44 and twice as fast." Victorious in events ranging from closed-course pylon to coast-to-coast transcontinental racing, the Patterson, Louisiana–based company was one of the most respected aviation companies in the 1930s. Although an endless procession of professional racing pilots stood in line to fly them, Jimmie Wedell and Harry Williams selected only a lucky handful for the task.

Clockwise, this page, from top:
John Worthen, chief pilot, managed flight schedules and served as Williams's personal pilot. He flew the *45* in national races (1934). (Photo courtesy of the Louisiana State Museum)

To the amazement of Harry Williams, tiny Mary Hazlip, an active pilot prior to the popularity of Amelia Earhart, set women's world speed records in his personal racer, the *92* (1933). (Photo courtesy of the Louisiana State Museum)

The *44* first flew in 1931 and was the most successful aircraft of the company, twice winning both the Thompson and Bendix National Air Racing Trophies (1934). (Photo courtesy of the Louisiana State Museum)

Jim Hazlip worked for the Shell Oil Company with James Doolittle. Hazlip made Harry Williams agree that if he won races in the *92,* his wife, Mary, would be allowed to fly it in the women's competitions (1933). (Photo courtesy of the Louisiana State Museum)

As skilled a pilot as his brother Jimmie, Walter Wedell had a role in the air service that grew beyond daily flying. He led the maintenance and support personnel caring for the aircraft (1934). (Photo courtesy of the Newman Collection, Earl K. Long Library, University of New Orleans)

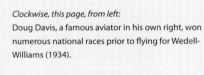

Clockwise, this page, from left:

Doug Davis, a famous aviator in his own right, won numerous national races prior to flying for Wedell-Williams (1934).

Lee Gehlbach flew the *92* for the air service following James Hazlip's retirement from racing. Gehlbach also flew the famous Gee-Bee Racers. Two years after Williams's death, Gehlbach was hired to fly the *92* for its new owner, Jack Wright, in the 1938 Bendix Trophy Race (1934).

The *45* introduced retractable landing gear. After Doug Davis's death, Williams donated the *45* to LSU's newly founded aeronautical engineering program. It was lost in a campus fire (1934).

Active through 1939, Roscoe Turner's Wedell-Williams racer is the only aircraft of the famous trio to survive and is now owned by the Cleveland Auto and Aviation Museum (1933).

The *92* was originally designed as a fast mail-carrying aircraft. Each racing season, Williams stepped aside, hiring professional pilots to fly it in tournaments across the United States. After four years in storage following its last race in 1938, it was donated to a World War II scrap-metal drive (1934). (Photos courtesy of the Louisiana State Museum)

Clockwise, this page, from left:
A pair of *44*s. Turner's racer featuring the golden paint scheme identifying its sponsor, "20th Century Pictures," beside Wedell's pristine racer in the 1933 air race lineup. (Photo courtesy of the Louisiana State Museum)

The *New 22* competed in the 1933 Los Angeles and 1934 Cleveland Air Races. It was built in partnership with the Delgado Trade School, School of Aviation, accounting for its similarity in design to the *Delgado Flash* (1933). (Photo courtesy of the Louisiana State Museum)

Harry P. Williams, shown here in the cockpit of his personal racer, the *92,* provided the financing and business sense necessary to operate the air service successfully (1932). (Photo courtesy of the Newman Collection, Earl K. Long Library, University of New Orleans)

The Wedell-Williams London-Melbourne Racer was not completed due to Jimmie Wedell's death just months before the event. A product of the Delgado partnership, this single-engine, long-range aircraft was of particular interest to Senator Huey P. Long (1934). (Photo courtesy of the Louisiana State Museum)

Jimmie Wedell, with only a ninth-grade education and blind in one eye, had a natural ability to understand and solve problems relative to speed and aerodynamics (1934). (Photo courtesy of the Louisiana State Museum)

Top left, Hazlip, Wedell, and Turner in front of their respective aircraft at the Thompson Trophy Race media event (1933). All built in Patterson, Louisiana. (Photo courtesy of the Louisiana State Museum)

Above, 1932 program. (Photo courtesy of the Louisiana State Museum)

Middle left, Turner's *121,* Williams's *92,* and Wedell's *44* prepare at the starting line (1933). (Photo courtesy of the Louisiana State Museum)

Above, Compact in size, the *We Will Jr.* wore three racing numbers: 17, 22, and 54. It was one of the first of Wedell's aircraft to fly, debuting in the 1930 All-American Derby and the Chicago National Air Races (1930). (Photo courtesy of the Louisiana State Museum)

Left, Jimmie Wedell fastening his parachute prior to a flight in the racer (1934). (Photo courtesy of the Newman Collection, Earl K. Long Library, University of New Orleans)

ROSCOE TURNER

Carelessly clad barnstorming flyers, sporting oil-stained jumpsuits and torn scarves as their principal badges of honor, served as aviation's ambassadors, until Corinth, Mississippi, native Roscoe Turner transformed the image of the profession. After serving in the U.S. Army Air Corps, Turner returned to civilian life, making a living as a nomadic barnstormer, traveling the post–World War I air show circuit with various partners and gaining notoriety.

Unlike his peers, Turner's unique stage presence, featuring the first tailored, impeccably clean civilian pilot uniform with lapelled wings, made a lasting impression on scores of spectators and built public confidence in a struggling "Wild West" environment. Initially, Turner was ridiculed by fellow aviators for asserting his personal belief that if pilots wanted to gain the respect of the public, rather than simply serve as entertainers, they had to present themselves appropriately. Turner's self-presentation, however, would transform the image of professional flying; his uniform design remains in use by airlines today.

Among Turner's chosen aircraft in this mission was a custom-built Wedell-Williams racer assembled especially for him in 1932 at the Patterson Airport. Turner delighted air show audiences across the United States as the first "Hollywood pilot" who earned his living promoting sponsors displayed across his aircraft fuselage. Accompanied by his mascot lion cub, Gilmore, Turner had charisma that gained the admiration of the director Howard Hughes as well as the famous leading ladies who accompanied him in countless publicity photographs and newsreels.

Throughout the 1930s, Turner became the undisputed master showman and "poster pilot" of the Golden Age of Aviation. His Wedell-Williams 121 racer was the symbol of speed and versatility. His endorsements included, among others, Heinz 57, Ring-Free Comet Motor Oil, and the Gilmore Oil Co. Turner was the first flying billboard, establishing licensing and promotions in a fashion similar to commercial endorsements by contemporary high-profile athletes and sporting events.

Turner, along with James Doolittle and Jimmie Wedell himself, dominated air racing headlines in the early 1930s. Turner was the first pilot to win both the Bendix and Thompson Trophy Races in the same year. He accomplished this feat in his custom Wedell-Williams Racer. However, these and other victories came with a price. Turner retired from racing at the end of the decade, surprised by his own luck after watching in horror as fellow flyers continued to perish in event-related accidents before his eyes.

During World War II, Turner established a flying school, the Roscoe Turner Aeronautical Company based in Indianapolis, Indiana, that trained thousands of cadet pilots for the U.S. Army Air Corps. After the war, he founded Turner Airlines, subsequently renamed Lake Central, which was absorbed by Northwest Airlines and is today operating as a part of Delta Airlines.

Turner remained aviation's elder ambassador until his death in 1970. Corinth named their general aviation airport the Roscoe Turner Airport in his honor.

Throughout the 1930s, Roscoe Turner relied on his Wedell-Williams Racer to attract public attention and a variety of sponsors. (Photo courtesy of the Louisiana State Museum)

Turner's skills as a showman and publicity artist attracted as many sponsors as his piloting. Here, his animal partner, Gilmore the Flying Lion, promotes the Gilmore Oil and Gasoline Company by parading through city streets in advance of a 1933 air race. (Photo courtesy of the Louisiana State Museum)

THE DELTA AIR SERVICE IN MONROE, LOUISIANA

Only a handful of airline names from the first one hundred years of air transport have become instantly recognizable to the public. One of the more prominent of these is Delta. Many of the company's more famous contemporaries, Eastern, Pan American, Trans World Airways (TWA), and Braniff, have faded into oblivion. From its first commercial passenger flight in 1929 through the shadows of World War II in 1941, Monroe, Louisiana, served as Delta's founding city and headquarters. Now based in Atlanta, Georgia, Delta is one of the world's largest and most influential commercial passenger carriers.

Visionary entrepreneur Collett Everman (C. E.) Woolman founded the airline. Woolman made Delta operations and service stand out by enforcing a strict code of customer service that became legendary in the airline industry. Woolman was one of the first airline executives to treat passengers as welcomed guests, emphasizing his belief that the company's survival was based on their return for another flight, a concept all but lost in an ever-expanding modern transportation industry.

By all accounts, Woolman's path to the helm of a major commercial airline is unique among industry executives. Woolman's father was a schoolteacher. As a young boy, he became fascinated by the insects that plagued the family property and nearby farmlands, a fascination that led to his majoring in entomology at the University of Illinois.

In 1909, Woolman participated in an internship in Europe. While in Reims, France, he attended an aerial exposition, one of the first primitive "air show" demonstrations of its kind. He watched as daredevils flew paper-thin aircraft overhead and the crowds reacted with exuberant fascination.

Woolman observed pilots flying approximately 200 feet above the crowd, making passes at low level and then circling the audience to make their way to the other end of the demonstration field. From that point, airplanes became his second passion. Shortly thereafter, he graduated from the University of Illinois.

Woolman began his career as an inspector for the U.S. Department of Agriculture (USDA) in Baton Rouge. He kept descriptive logbooks recording the effects of insects on farmlands, identifying a devastating phenomenon that was steadily increasing in magnitude: In the early twentieth century, nearly half of all farm products were threatened, contaminated, or completely destroyed by crop-eating insects and rodents.

In response, calcium arsenate, a key insecticide used by southern farmers, was applied manually to fields. This method did not successfully deter encroaching pests, most notably the boll weevil, in the cotton fields of north Louisiana. Damage to farmlands was so serious that the pest became a cultural centerpiece in the popular music of the era.

Woolman theorized that applying the chemical from the air, or "dusting" the field, would be far more effective. The U.S. Army Air Corps loaned Woolman aircraft that he promptly modified to spray select fields. Woolman instructed the pilots on how to drop the chemicals over a target crop, and ground teams monitored the effect. When it was determined that damage to "dusted" fields was measurably less than on fields treated by manual methods, "crop-dusting" was born.

In 1925, Woolman was hired into the private sector by the Huff-Daland Company of Macon, Georgia, a private firm intent on capitalizing on the dusting innovation. Within a year, he had convinced the owners to relocate to Monroe, Louisiana. From there, the company served farmers throughout the entire Southeast. In 1926, the govern-

ment of Peru invited Huff-Daland to operate a dusting service in South America. Over the next several years, under Woolman's direction, the aircraft served the southeastern United States during its growing season and then relocated to South America in domestic downtime.

While in Peru, Woolman became interested in transporting mail and passengers by air from remote communities to populated cities. Another South American operation in its infancy—Pan American–Grace Airways (Panagra), partially owned by Pan American Airways, most notably its president, Juan Trippe—set out to dominate passenger and airmail routes throughout Central and South America. Trippe kept a watchful eye on Woolman's growing interest in Peru and in a series of political moves all but ensured that Huff-Daland did not obtain airmail or passenger routes in South or Central America. The

Above, In 1945, Delta purchased surplus Stearman military trainers to upgrade its fleet of crop-dusters.

Opposite left, Delta Airlines was founded on this grass field in Monroe, Louisiana (1929).

Opposite right, Delta Air Service often hosted air shows to demonstrate aerobatics and dusting techniques to local residents (1930). (Photos courtesy of the Delta Air Transport Heritage Museum)

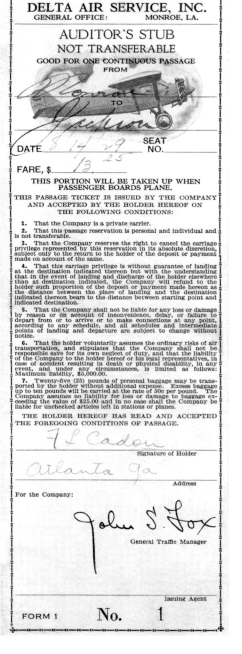

Above, Seen here in late 1929, Delta Airlines' original headquarters building was constructed on Selman Field in Monroe. A memorial erected by supporters of the Delta Air Transport Heritage Museum now stands on its original abandoned foundation.

Far right, This airline passenger ticket issued by Delta Air Service on August 14, 1929, was for travel between Monroe, Louisiana, and Jackson, Mississippi.

Right, Delta's 1929 brochure for its first flight.

Opposite left, Two of Delta's first passengers prepare to board in Monroe (1929).

Opposite right, The Delta Air Service flight schedule from 1929. (Photos courtesy of the Delta Air Transport Heritage Museum)

DELTA AIR SERVICE, Inc.

General Offices—Monroe, Louisiana. Tel. 1631

OFFICERS

D. Y. Smith, President
C. E. Woolman, Vice-President and General Manager
Captain Harold R. Harris, Vice-President
Travis Oliver, Secretary-Treasurer
J. S. Fox, General Traffic Manager

TABLE 83   DALLAS—JACKSON

Read Down		(Daily)		Read Up
8 30	Lv..........................	Dallas	.........................Ar	4 00
10 50	Lv..........................	Shreveport	Lv	1 45
11 50	Ar..........................	Monroe	Lv	12 15
12 15	Lv..........................	Monroe	.........................Ar	11 50
1 30	Ar..........................	Jackson	Lv	10 30

FARES

			Dallas	Shreveport	Monroe
Shreveport....................	O. W.		$21.50	......	......
	R. T.		38.00	......	......
Monroe......................	O. W.		34.00	$12.50	......
	R. T.		63.00	20.00	......
Jackson......................	O. W.		47.25	25.75	$13.25
	R. T.		90.00	46.50	21.50

Baggage Allowance—25 pounds free. Excess at 25c per pound.

ensuing politics eventually forced Huff-Daland to withdraw from the region. Panagra progressively monopolized the South American operation, and Woolman remembered Trippe's cutthroat business tactics for the rest of his career.

To Woolman's amazement when he returned to the United States, Huff-Daland executives had decided to sell the domestic dusting operation. To counter the move, Woolman recruited Louisiana-based financiers to purchase the company, allowing it to remain in Monroe. The operation was renamed the Delta Air Service.

The dusting fleet had grown to eighteen aircraft, and Woolman positioned the Monroe operation to include airmail and passenger service. Limited startup capital inhibited the purchase of new aircraft. John Fox, a private aircraft owner in Bastrop, Louisiana, accepted stock in the new operation in exchange for his aircraft, a six-passenger Travel Air S-6000-B.

On June 17, 1929, Delta Air Service carried its first paying passengers on a route between Dallas, Texas; Shreveport and Monroe, Louisiana; and Jackson, Mississippi. Crop-dusting continued, but Woolman now embarked upon building an airline. The route soon expanded to include Birmingham and Atlanta. Much like Harry Williams in south Louisiana, Woolman had two critical missions. First, he had to convince travelers, the majority of whom had never flown before, to use the new service. Second, and far more financially rewarding, he had to win the coveted federal airmail routes within his territory to reinforce revenues.

Initially, Postmaster Walter F. Brown (1929–33) believed that only large companies could provide the reliable service necessary for carrying airmail. Whether this epiphany was one he reached on his own or through the influence of up-and-coming aviation entrepreneurs who were intent on dominating the new route system is often debated. Unfortunately for Woolman, Delta was a small operation, and, like many small companies across the country that were capable of catering to regional communities, it did not appeal to Brown.

In June 1930, the U.S. Post Office created a new mail route along Delta's flight path between Dallas and Birmingham, and the contract went, not to Delta, but to a larger competitor, American Airways Corporation. American attracted the attention of Postmaster Brown by buying up smaller airlines the size of Delta that operated throughout the country. Ironically, Woolman had refused an early purchase offer made by American Airways. The company relied on revenues from crop-dusting while Woolman planned his next move.

In late 1933, President Franklin Delano Roosevelt's postmaster general, William Farley, initiated a new bidding process for airmail contracts. However, there is reason to suspect that early delays associated

This Travel Air S-600-B, restored in Delta's original paint scheme to resemble its first aircraft, once flew at air shows throughout the country. It is now safely preserved on static display at the Delta Air Transport Heritage Museum. (Photo courtesy of the Delta Air Transport Heritage Museum)

Delta began service to New Orleans in 1943 at the request of the War Department to assist in transporting personnel between New Orleans, Alexandria, and Shreveport. Three years later, in 1946, it relocated operations to the new Moisant International Airport (MSY). (Photo courtesy of the Louisiana Division, City Archives and Special Collections, New Orleans Public Library)

with awards to Delta, similar to those handicapping Wedell-Williams, were driven by Roosevelt's reluctance to assist companies that might be potential supporters of Long's presidential ambitions.

In the years following Long's 1935 assassination, Delta repositioned itself on a path to prosperity. The airline attracted larger southern investors, including the tobacco entrepreneur R. J. Reynolds. Woolman purchased new Lockheed 10A Electra aircraft and in 1939 acquired Douglas DC-3 airliners.

Reynolds provided capital for Delta's pre–World War II growth and enhanced its image among business travelers throughout the southeastern United States. Soon after investing in the airline, Reynolds demanded that Woolman move the company to Atlanta, a larger city with a more diversified economy. The relocation was completed in March 1941. Out of respect for tradition, Delta Airlines continued to hold its annual stockholders meetings in Monroe through the end of the twentieth century. The concrete foundation of the original Delta Headquarters Building at the Monroe Airport, though masked by an overgrowth of trees, is proudly identified with a plaque erected by the Delta Air Transport Heritage Museum.

During World War II, all U.S. airlines were pressed into military service to transport troops on domestic routes. After the war, Delta's commercial routes expanded rapidly. Under Woolman's direction, Delta was the first airline in American aviation history to introduce three different models of commercial jets into U.S. passenger service. These aircraft were the Douglas DC-8 in September 1959; the Convair 880, the world's fastest transcontinental jetliner, in May 1960; and in December 1965, the Douglas DC-9, the first medium-range jetliner. One of the first scheduled flights of the Convair 880 jet was between New Orleans Moisant and New York Idlewild (now JFK International) Airports.

Delta has navigated a volatile industry and emerged the survivor of numerous mergers with other airlines, absorbing other profitable carriers over the years, including Chicago and Southern, Northeastern, Western, and, most recently, Northwest Airlines.

Among that number is also Juan Trippe's Pan American Airlines, which declared bankruptcy in 1991. As PanAm's pilots prepared to park their aircraft for the last time, Delta's board of directors stepped in and purchased the company. In very short order, Delta delivered a knockout punch to Pan American, the company that sixty years earlier had deprived it of success in the South American market. In an ironic reversal of fortune, Woolman's contemporaries shut down the Pan American operation and liquidated what remained of Juan Trippe's assets.

Delta's contemporary domestic network provides service to all fifty states, accompanied by international routes reaching every continent. Today Delta Airlines operates a fleet of more than one thousand jet aircraft.

Above, This 1960 publicity photograph, taken at "MSY," was used by Delta to promote the new jet service in New Orleans. (Photo courtesy of the Louisiana Division, City Archives and Special Collections, New Orleans Public Library)

Above right, On May 15, 1960, Delta became the second airline to introduce jet service to Louisiana residents with the Convair 880. On domestic routes, the aircraft could outfly the Boeing 707 and the Douglas DC-8, but at a cost. The 880 burned more fuel and was not equipped for transoceanic flight as were its competitors. (Photo courtesy of the Louisiana Division, City Archives and Special Collections, New Orleans Public Library)

Right, The *Spirit of Delta,* a $50 million Boeing 767–200, was purchased by the employees for their company via payroll deduction in the early 1980s. Retired from the fleet, *Spirit* is displayed in the Delta Air Transport Heritage Museum. (Photo courtesy of the Delta Air Transport Heritage Museum)

This memorial stands at the entrance of Monroe Regional Airport (MLU), honoring the founding of Delta Air Service, today Delta Airlines, there in 1929. (Photo by the author)

By December 2010, Monroe Regional Airport operated the last of the 1960s-style airline terminals in Louisiana. Construction of its contemporary replacement had begun approximately four months earlier. (Photo by the author)

COLLETT EVERMAN "C. E." WOOLMAN

Collett Everman Woolman, pictured here before the commercial jet era of the early 1950s, founded Delta Air Service on an accurate hunch that businesspersons traveling from Dallas and Atlanta, as well as cities in between, would pay the extra cost in airfare in the interest of saving time (1950). (Photo courtesy of the Delta Air Transport Heritage Museum)

C. E. Woolman was a rare breed among early airline entrepreneurs, serving the company in that capacity for thirty-six years. He had the gift of being able to recall the names of all of his employees throughout the early years of the airline's development. He regularly shared the story of the company's humble origins as a crop-dusting operation in north Louisiana in a style that the employees could identify with, making them feel as if they were a part of something special. The company thrives in no small measure due to the early corporate foundation put in place by this inspired leader.

CHAPTER THREE

SKIES FIT FOR A KINGFISH

SHUSHAN AIRPORT

Governor Huey P. Long hoped to achieve his ambition to win the White House in the 1936 presidential election. As a means of achieving this goal, he intended to transform Louisiana into a symbol of post-Depression recovery, an advanced utopia where "none should be too poor and none should be too rich, and every comfort and convenience known to man would be provided."

A number of options for building a state-owned public airport in the city of New Orleans were explored. Governor and Senator-elect Long made it clear to the residents of the Crescent City that while he fully supported construction of a much-needed modern airport, he had no intention of allowing the New Orleans–based anti-Long factions access to its control.

Folklore suggests that Abraham L. Shushan, one of Long's closest confidants and president of the Orleans Levee District, pledged to the governor that an airport could be built on "reclaimed land" pumped from the bottom of Lake Pontchartrain to create a state-owned peninsula, thereby depriving the city's administration of any authority in operating the facility or reaping its revenues. Impressed with his lieutenant's ingenuity, Long instructed him to make it a masterpiece, and to name it the Shushan Airport.

Construction of the massive Shushan Airport seawall (1930). (Photo courtesy of the Abe L. Shushan Collection, Earl K. Long Library, University of New Orleans)

Planning for the Shushan Airport began soon after the election of Governor Huey P. Long. Once work on the massive landfill was completed, construction of the two art deco hangars and the air terminal building began (1932). (Photo courtesy of the Abe L. Shushan Collection, Earl K. Long Library, University of New Orleans)

Although New Orleans mayor Semmes Walmsley was bombarded with petitions from the local business community to build a public airport closer to New Orleans, he dismissed Shushan's proposal that a landfill project currently under way creating Lakeshore Drive could be expanded to accommodate a new airport, preferring instead to have the facility built within city jurisdiction.

Other anti-Long opponents also objected, citing original legislation that divided the lakeshore into five zones, known as "reaches," and prohibited work on more than three of the zones at any given time to prevent congestion. Long called a special session and had the legislation amended to allow work on the airport to begin immediately.

A triangular-shaped landfill within an approximately one square mile area was created from earth pumped out of the lake bottom and encased in a concrete seawall peninsula extending off the southeastern shore of the lake. Sparing no expense and under the direction of Governor-turned-Senator Long, Shushan ensured that the magnitude of the landfill was matched by the beauty of the terminal building and hangars constructed on it. Each structure was ornately crafted and adorned in art deco splendor.

Eight aviation murals by the artist Xavier Gonzalez were commissioned and displayed on a second-floor balcony promenade in the terminal building. Every corner of the building was crafted by WPA artisans, featuring designs within the molding, ironworks, the centerpiece compass rose, and the accompanying marble staircase. Abe Shushan's initials were prominently engraved in many of these features.

A sculptured "Fountain of Four Winds" and an Olympic-size public swimming pool were also planned and later built in front of the two hangars. Following years of construction, Shushan Airport was officially dedicated the week of February 9, 1934. Abe Shushan and Governor Oscar K. Allen, successor to Long, flew to the field from the Baton Rouge Airport and received an artillery salute upon arrival.

As part of the festivities, the Pan American Air Races were established and planned as an annual event on the field. The inaugural race lasted through the following Sunday, February 18, and featured several famous racing pilots including Jimmie Wedell, who flew to victory in the 100-kilometer competition with his new aircraft the 45. Retired racing pioneer James Doolittle participated in the ribbon-cutting ceremony.

The opening ceremonies were not without incident. Thunderstorms delayed the events. While landing following a stunt-flying exhibition, pilot "Captain" Merle Nelson crashed on the new runway. Nelson survived the impact unscratched but was trapped in the wreckage. During Nelson's attempt to escape, the aircraft exploded, burning him to death in full view of the shocked spectators. On the final day of the races, February 18, parachute jumper Ben Grew, and his pilot, Charles Kenily, were killed when Grew's chute opened prematurely and became tangled on the tail of the airplane, freezing all controls

Shushan Airport's runways were actively used by pilots long before the dedication ceremony in February 1934. In this Wedell-Williams Air Service publicity photograph, the far-from-completed air terminal building can be seen in the background. (Photo courtesy of the Newman Collection, Earl K. Long Library, University of New Orleans)

and plunging them into Lake Pontchartrain just off the end of the runway. The novelist William Faulkner, who was in attendance, was so moved by having witnessed the fatalities that he put aside work on his pending novel *Absalom, Absalom!* to write "Pylon," a story based on the opening of Shushan Airport and the pilots participating in the Pan American Air Races.

The airport served New Orleans as Shushan Airport until 1940, when the name was changed to the New Orleans Airport following Abe Shushan's conviction on income tax and mail fraud. In a lighter moment following his conviction, Shushan told reporters that it would take just as long to remove his initials from everything in the terminal, including the molding, compass rose, and doorknobs, as it did to build the entire airfield.

The airport was home to Army Air Corps units through World War II; they shared the facility with commercial airline operations until mid-1946, when the air carriers relocated to Moisant Airport in Kenner. Upon departure of the airlines, the airport functioned exclusively as a general and business aviation airport.

In 1964, the Orleans Levee Board remodeled the terminal building. The artwork, sculptures, and classic art deco designs were covered in place to make room for additional offices and meeting areas. Thick, windowless plates were incorporated into the new exterior design so that the original terminal building could be used as a state nuclear fallout shelter. The primary runway was lengthened to 6,900 feet, and the facility was renamed the New Orleans Lakefront Airport. It hosted annual air shows for the City of New Orleans. During Saints games and other major sports events, it became the ground operations center for Goodyear blimp flights.

Throughout the 1960s and 1970s, attempts by the Orleans Levee Board to revive limited commercial airline service were unsuccessful. One such initiative during the early days of the space program requested authority from the Civil Aeronautics Board (CAB) for Southern Airways to operate a daily flight between the New Orleans Lakefront and the Huntsville, Alabama, Airports. The flights would have eased regular commuting of NASA employees between the Michoud Assembly Facility in New Orleans East and Huntsville's Marshall Spaceflight Center. The route was tentatively approved by the CAB, but Southern elected not to inaugurate the flights, maintaining a consolidated operation at Moisant Airport. In 1979, following deregulation of the airline industry, the Orleans Levee Board unsuccessfully attempted to lure the then eight-year-old Southwest Airlines to Lakefront Airport as a location for introducing service to New Orleans.

Above, A 1934 aerial view of the Shushan Airport.

Left, The seaplane ramp opened in 1933 on the east end of the field, making Shushan Airport the first facility to combine amphibious and land-based aircraft operations within a single airport. (Photos courtesy of the Abe L. Shushan Collection, Earl K. Long Library, University of New Orleans)

Lakefront has earned a reputation for catering to large volumes of aircraft traffic generated by such high-profile events as the Super Bowl, the Sugar Bowl, Mardi Gras, and industry conventions. Although located within the air traffic approach-and-departure control area of New Orleans International, proximity allows business and general aviation passengers to avoid delays associated with commercial airline operations.

New revenue streams from such sources as additional office buildings and the Star Casino Complex, later Bally's Casino, built at the site of the original seaplane base, changed the facility's east wall footprint and complemented utility. The airport became a regular, favored venue for the National Business Aviation Association (NBAA), attracting more than three hundred display aircraft and thirty-five thousand visitors on-site to one of the largest aircraft sales conventions in the world.

In August 2005, over 80 percent of the Lakefront Airport infrastructure was damaged or completely destroyed by Hurricane Katrina. In the years following the storm, a massive rebuilding effort was funded by FEMA, FAA airport-improvement grants, insurance coverage, and private investment. Bally's Casino did not reopen after the storm.

Most notable—and undoubtedly the grand unforeseen benefit to come from the losses the airport suffered in the devastation—was the restoration of the Shushan Terminal Building to its original grandeur. In 2009, a $12 million restoration was begun. What remained of the large gray plates encasing the Shushan Terminal Building was removed. After years of neglect, nearly all of the original outdoor artwork was refurbished. The rear porticos demolished in the 1964 renovation have been replaced. The extraneous office space in the interior was gutted. The WPA molding and artwork that had been hidden by the "modern" renovation has been exposed again.

The two original accompanying hangars have also been repaired, reawakening the terminal complex as one of the only restored first-generation (1930–35) art deco airports in continuous operation from the Golden Age of Aviation. New Orleans Lakefront Airport remains an active general aviation facility capable of accommodating the largest business aircraft operating today.

Opposite, This 1934 aerial photograph of the Shushan Terminal (*center*), Moffett Hangar (*left*), and Lindbergh Hangar (*right*) reveals the absence of the Fountain of Four Winds and the Olympic-size swimming pool, which were added the following year as WPA projects.

Above, Aerial photograph of the dedication ceremony at Shushan Airport on February 9, 1934. (Photos courtesy of the Abe L. Shushan Collection, Earl K. Long Library, University of New Orleans)

This page:

Left, This 1934 hardcover book celebrating the opening was given to VIP guests. (Photograph courtesy of the Louisiana State Museum)

Bottom left, The opening celebration of the airport produced numerous mementos. (Artifact courtesy of the Louisiana State Museum; photo by the author)

Bottom right, This badge was worn by the airport field service staff during the 1934 opening festivities. (Artifact courtesy of the Louisiana State Museum; photo by the author)

Opposite page:

Top, Shushan Airport Terminal Building landside entrance, facing south (1934). (Photo courtesy of the Abe L. Shushan Collection, Earl K. Long Library, University of New Orleans)

Bottom left, The airport's original dedication plaque is on display at the University of New Orleans, Louisiana and Special Collections, Earl K. Long Library. (Photo courtesy of the Abe L. Shushan Collection, Earl K. Long Library, University of New Orleans)

Bottom right, Abe Shushan—accompanied by Governor Oscar K. Allen, Richard Leche (*rear*), and New Orleans mayor Semmes Walmsley—watches the air show and Pan American Air Races during the February 1934 dedication. (Photo courtesy of the Abe L. Shushan Collection, Earl K. Long Library, University of New Orleans)

Above, Airside of the Shushan Terminal Building and entrance for arriving passengers as it appeared between 1934 and 1946.

Above right, The artwork over the east terminal entrance features a 1933 National Recovery Act eagle as its centerpiece. Also note the intricate sculptures featured on the portico. This doorway was used to isolate inbound international passengers in a waiting room prior to customs clearance.

Right, The original terminal featured two airside porticos for persons to await arriving and departing aircraft. During the 1964 renovations, both were demolished; however, the left portico's foundation was extended to expand the airport's restaurant facilities. (Photos courtesy of the Abe L. Shushan Collection, Earl K. Long Library, University of New Orleans)

The Shushan Terminal entrance of 1934 features extensive masonry artwork, including the depiction of Icarus of Greek mythology, who flew too close to the sun. (Photo courtesy of the Abe L. Shushan Collection, Earl K. Long Library, University of New Orleans)

Right, A rare 1934 pre-dedication photograph of an American Airways Curtiss Condor and a Wedell-Williams Air Service Lockheed Vega. These passenger aircraft were the staple of airline fleets in the early 1930s prior to the introduction of the Douglas DC-3.

Below, A Chicago and Southern Lockheed Electra awaits passengers for its return trip in to the Windy City in 1935. The aircraft made seven stops on its return trip to Chicago, including Jackson and Greenwood, Mississippi; Memphis, Tennessee; St. Louis, Missouri; and Springfield and Peoria, Illinois. (Photos courtesy of the Louisiana State Library)

After World War II, general aviation leisure flying was more commonplace at the Lake Pontchartrain field, as evidenced by this postwar photograph of an Aeronca aircraft preparing for flight. (Photo courtesy of the Louisiana State Museum)

Left, The Shushan Air Terminal interior lobby is a treasure trove of unique WPA artisan craftsmanship, much of which still survives (1934).

Bottom left, The air terminal's second floor features a series of eight murals by the artist Xavier Gonzalez. With the theme of global aviation, the collection serves as the centerpiece of the terminal's lounge area. Accompanied by oversized windows providing bird's-eye views of the flight activity outside on the runways, the subjects inspired passengers living though the harsh Depression years to contemplate the hope and wonders of flying (1934).

Opposite, The lobby's marble staircase led passengers and awaiting party members to the grand second-story open balcony (1934). (Photos courtesy of the Abe L. Shushan Collection, Earl K. Long Library, University of New Orleans)

Right, The Walnut Room instantly became a popular banquet facility for elegant occasions, including wedding receptions, political meetings, and carnival club functions. Occupying the first floor's entire west wing, the original 1934 design seen here featured a balcony accessed by the second floor that was used by featured guests and speechmakers.

Bottom, The small café on the terminal's first floor featured one of the last works by the artist Alexander John Drysdale, a mural of a south Louisiana marsh landscape. Unfortunately, the work was lost through a series of facility renovations (1934). (Photos courtesy of the Abe L. Shushan Collection, Earl K. Long Library, University of New Orleans)

ABE L. SHUSHAN

Whether by chance or masterfully executed planning, by 1934, the Orleans Levee Board president Abraham L. Shushan had unquestionably become a critical catalyst of early air transportation in Louisiana—and for a time, at least, one of U.S. aviation's most visible advocates. The Shushan Airport in New Orleans was, through the era of the Great Depression and World War II, one of the most emulated aviation complexes in the United States.

Shushan incorporated the energies of nationally renowned airline executives Eddie Rickenbacker (Eastern Airlines) and C. R. Smith (American Airways) as well as local entrepreneurs James Wedell and Harry Williams (Wedell-Williams Air Service) into his campaign to build a first-class airport for the state. A native of St. John the Baptist Parish, Shushan entered politics in 1920, when Governor John Parker appointed the twenty-seven-year-old to the Orleans Levee Board. His appointment continued under Governors Fuqua and Simpson. Governor Huey P. Long, elected in 1928, recognized Shushan's political shrewdness, and the pair quickly became confidants. Long ensured Shushan's appointment to president of the Orleans Levee Board in 1929.

In addition to the airport once bearing his name, the Lake Pontchartrain seawall and its accompanying massive landfill (creating the Lakeview subdivisions) were completed under Shushan's administration. The euphoria attending these accomplishments was short-lived. Long was assassinated the following year, and Shushan was the first member of Long's inner circle to be pursued and indicted by federal agents. In 1940, he was charged with income tax evasion and mail fraud and then imprisoned. Years later, Shushan was pardoned by President Harry S. Truman.

Following the conviction, the airfield was renamed the New Orleans Airport. One state senator comically suggested the airport be renamed after someone or something whose name started with an *S* rather than continue the expensive work of removing Shushan's imprint.

Following Truman's pardon, Shushan retired to a private life on the Lake Pontchartrain North Shore. He watched in horror in 1963 and 1964 as the beautiful art deco airport terminal building he championed was remodeled into a fallout shelter and "contemporary" office building. Abe Shushan died in 1966 at the age of seventy, two years after the renovation of the airport terminal building had completely transformed his namesake's appearance.

Above, Many believe that Abe Shushan, sound businessman and sharp-witted politician (*left*), pictured here in 1934 with Captain Eddie Rickenbacker, president of Eastern Airlines, sacrificed his own career to help Governor Long maintain his high-profile public image in the hostile anti-Long stronghold of New Orleans.

Left, Abe Shushan accompanies Senator Long during a formal welcoming ceremony onboard a naval vessel docked in the Port of New Orleans in 1933. (Photos courtesy of the Abe L. Shushan Collection, Earl K. Long Library, University of New Orleans)

THE MOFFETT AND LINDBERGH/WILLIAMS AIRCRAFT HANGARS

Accompanying the opulent Shushan Terminal are two identical aircraft hangars constructed on either side of the main building. Oversized for their day, each structure had been specifically designed in anticipation of large modern aircraft being produced by manufacturers such as Boeing, Consolidated, and Douglas. The hangars were named in honor of U.S. Navy Rear Admiral William Adger Moffett, often called the "father of naval aviation," and Charles Lindbergh, the first man to fly solo across the Atlantic Ocean, in 1927.

When Rear Admiral Moffett died in the crash of the dirigible (naval blimp) USS *Akron* on April 4, 1933, the hangar to the left of the Shushan Terminal Building was formally dedicated to Moffett's lifetime of service to naval aviation.

In 1938, Charles Lindbergh's highly publicized, spirited meeting with Adolph Hitler and Hermann Goering in Germany just prior to World War II resulted in him being discredited as a Nazi sympathizer. Shortly thereafter, his name was removed from the hangar, and it was officially renamed for the recently deceased Harry P. Williams, founder of the Wedell-Williams Air Service.

Today these original hangars, along with the restored terminal building, make up a one-of-a-kind trio, the rarest of surviving aviation landmarks from the Golden Age of Aviation.

Above left, Admiral William Adger Moffett, known as "the father of naval aviation" (1918). (Photo courtesy of the Louisiana State Museum)

Above right, The Lindbergh Hangar (renamed in 1938 for Harry P. Williams) to the right of the terminal was used for commercial airline operations, including airmail flights by American Airways. (Photo courtesy of the Abe L. Shushan Collection, Earl K. Long Library, University of New Orleans)

Below right, This 1934 photograph of the Moffett Hangar illustrates the enormous size of the bays. Each hangar was capable of sheltering three DC-3 airliners, the largest aircraft of this golden age. (Photo courtesy of the Abe L. Shushan Collection, Earl K. Long Library, University of New Orleans)

RUCKINS D. "BO" McKNEELY AND AMELIA EARHART

One of the most famous early patrons of Shushan Airport was the aviator Amelia Earhart. During her ill-fated attempt to circumnavigate the world by air in the summer of 1937, she used the airport on Lake Pontchartrain as an overnight rest stop. On the evening of Saturday, May 22, 1937, her aircraft was secured in one of the original terminal hangars. Earhart and her party spent the night in the airport hotel suite located on the second floor of the east wing of the terminal.

Though her stay was unannounced, it leaked to the local media, who publicized her visit in the following day's paper as a "test flight." Earhart had actually begun the historic journey three days earlier in Oakland, California. New Orleans was her second overnight stop on the planned around-the-world adventure, and the flight was officially announced in Miami, Florida, two days later, following her departure from the mainland and the reach of the paparazzi.

On these first legs across the United States, Earhart was accompanied by her mechanic, Ruckins D. "Bo" McKneely, a native of Patterson, Louisiana, and the former lead mechanic for the Wedell-Williams Air Service. McKneely was considered an expert on Lockheed aircraft, the type Earhart selected for use on her flight around the world.

McKneely had previously maintained the Wedell-Williams airliners and Harry P. Williams's personal aircraft collection in Patterson, but he resigned from the company following Jimmie Wedell's death. McKneely moved to California and went to work for the Lockheed Aircraft Corporation. Earhart knew McKneely from his work with Jimmie Wedell, and after his settling in California, she asked him to be her personal mechanic. McKneely accepted the offer and was instrumental in preparing Earhart's Lockheed Electra aircraft for the long journey, overseeing installation of additional fuel tanks and other necessary overwater equipment.

Earhart's global flight was originally planned to carry two vital passengers, McKneely, who would serve as mechanic, and radio operator/navigator Harry Manning. However, just before the journey began, Harry Manning, who had frequent, often harsh disagreements

with Earhart's husband, the publicist George Putnam, was replaced with the veteran Pan American Airlines navigator Fred Noonan. In an interesting connection to Louisiana aviation, in 1929 and 1930, Noonan had lived briefly in New Orleans and obtained his commercial pilot's license at Menefee Airport under the tutelage of airmail operator Southern Air Transport Company. Prior to flying with Earhart, Noonan became a respected expert navigator, working with Charles Lindbergh during the mapping of the Pacific air routes for Pan American Airways.

In May 1937, McKneely's father, who still lived in Patterson, was in poor health. Upon arriving in New Orleans during the overnight stay at Shushan Airport, McKneely learned that his father's condition was more serious than he had known. After considerable personal debate, McKneely advised Earhart that he wanted to remain behind to assist the family. Earhart agreed, which left her with a single, new crewmember, Noonan, who had not participated in the flight preparations from the initial planning stages. McKneely had planned on meeting her again at the completion of the flight in Oakland, California, the following month.

Following the aircraft's disappearance in Pacific waters, McKneely struggled with a lifetime of self-imposed guilt, blaming himself for Earhart's fate. In spite of endless speculative interpretations by fortune seekers, the facts strongly support that Earhart ran out of fuel fewer than one hundred miles from her destination, Howland Island. Following the unsuccessful search, McKneely refused to discuss Earhart's disappearance with anyone, including his own family members. McKneely spent the remainder of his career working on special projects for Lockheed Aircraft Company. Only very late in life, within two years of his death, did he openly express the depth of his feelings about the disappearance of his friend. McKneely was convinced that had he been on board, because of his familiarity with the aircraft's performance, he could have stretched the fuel range and successfully completed the flight.

Above left, Bo McKneely of Patterson, Louisiana, was Amelia Earhart's personal mechanic. He was scheduled to ride with her on her attempt to fly around the world but changed his plans due to his father's illness (1937). (Photo courtesy of Gwen McKneely Carter)

CHAPTER FOUR

TRANSFORMATIONS

Following the defeat of the Axis powers in 1945, the United States was left with a military surplus of arms and airplanes. Accompanying the fruits of victory was a home front with an abundance of vacant military airfields and bases throughout the country.

Civilian airports commandeered by the War Department were returned to their owners. Considerable military infrastructure, including hangars, offices, maintenance equipment, and hard-surfaced runways, was left in place on these properties. Louisiana, hosting its share of these home-front operations, amassed a sizable inventory of well-equipped airfields that provided a foundation for the postwar growth of civil aviation.

Much like the demobilization following World War II, several of Louisiana's Cold War military airfields transitioned into viable civilian facilities after the fall of the Iron Curtain. Two of the most prominent examples are England Air Park in Alexandria and Chennault International Airport in Lake Charles. These airfields supported the strategic, tactical, and logistical air operations of the U.S. Army Air Corps and U.S. Air Force from the onset of the Second World War through the end of the Soviet Union's control of Eastern Europe.

When the Department of Defense closes or consolidates base operations, the impact on local economies can be devastating. The communities of central and southwestern Louisiana established the infrastructure to maintain civil operations at these former military air bases. Each has become an important economic engine for area citizens and a national benchmark for military-to-civilian property transition.

Moisant Hangar's busy interior in the mid-1950s. (Photo courtesy of the Louisiana State Museum)

Louisiana's prewar civilian airports had been absorbed into the military airfield network for the support of training and stateside patrols. Unique among U.S. states, Louisiana was home to key petroleum manufacturing, shipping, and staging for overseas transport. The Mississippi River and the Gulf of Mexico played a pivotal role in providing support and materials that led to victory.

Regions of the state were mobilized for different roles. To the north, Barksdale Army Air Field (now Barksdale Air Force Base) was home to bombing and fighter squadrons that over the course of the war fought on both fronts. Barksdale also served as an important route stop for transcontinental military traffic. In Monroe, Selman Field was home to a large training base for navigators and bombardiers.

To the south, Houma-Terrebonne Airport and the naval base built in New Iberia, today's Acadiana Regional Airport, supported continuous patrols of the mouth of the Mississippi River and the Gulf of Mexico. "Lighter-than-air" Navy blimps based at the Houma Naval Air Station performed surveillance and spotting missions for PBY Catalina patrol squadrons from across the coastal protection network. In New Orleans, Shushan Airport housed a bomber wing and Moisant "Army Airfield" supported fighter units.

In central Louisiana, England and Esler Army Airfields and a number of other smaller bases catered to troop training and transport operations. At the end of hostilities, communities that had no public airport prior to the war suddenly found themselves inheriting decommissioned facilities at a minimal cost to local taxpayers.

Still other Louisiana communities had both military and commercial airfields in place prior to the war. In such cases the military airfield, having built upon its original infrastructure during the conflict, usually remained active with the armed services, while the associated civilian airport that had served as an outlying field, after receiving welcome upgrades under the command of the U.S. Army Air Corps or U.S. Navy, was returned to the municipal owner.

Moisant/Louis Armstrong International Airport—New Orleans

The idea of constructing a new airport in New Orleans, owned and operated by the city, rather than continuing to depend on the state for air service at the former Shushan Airport was proposed in 1940 by Douglas O. Langstaff, a partner in the Chapman & Langstaff Flying

Service originally based at the Wedell-Williams Airport in Jefferson. Langstaff founded the Association of Commerce, a professional group that became the New Orleans Aviation Board in 1943. The association set its sights on 650 acres of farmland along Highway 61 (Airline Highway) in neighboring Kenner, a community supporting a modest population of 1,500. The City of New Orleans received an $800,000 grant from the Civil Aeronautics Administration (CAA) to clear the area and begin construction on two 5,000-foot runways.

Because of the Japanese attack on Pearl Harbor in December 1941, the U.S. Army Air Corps occupied the uncompleted airfield only two months after construction began. Numerous wartime projects, including two additional runways, were initiated and paid for by the War Department. When the airfield was returned to the city, it featured one of the most up-to-date infrastructures in the country, lacking only a public airport terminal building. The official dedication took place in January 1946, at which time the airport was formally named Moisant International in honor of the flyer John Bevins Moisant. The use of Moisant's name had been suggested from the beginning of the project.

The air racing champion General James Doolittle, who was present for the opening of Shushan but was now more famous for his courageous raid on Tokyo in April 1942, presided over the ceremony. The six airlines serving New Orleans—Pan American Airways, National Airlines, Eastern, Chicago & Southern, Delta, and Mid-Continent Airlines—relocated their operations to the new facility in April and May. An abandoned Air Corps hangar, lacking air-conditioning and affectionately remembered for its leaking roofs, was used as the "temporary" passenger terminal. It would take thirteen years for a permanent replacement to be operational on the airport.

The new terminal, opening in 1959, was one of the largest in the nation, with spacious ticketing areas for airlines; such amenities as fine dining, gift shops, and conference rooms supported by two "piers" (the original name used for airport concourses); and an attached eagle-nest air traffic control tower. Considering the luxurious surroundings of the Shushan Terminal, its long-awaited opening provided welcome relief to both airlines and passengers alike. Today, the last remaining remnant of the original structure—its trademark Parabola section—is easily distinguished from more recent construction that has overtaken the original design.

That same year, airlines increased service to south Louisiana via the Southern Transcontinental Air Route, a progressive expansion of

Moisant Airport used surplus Air Corps hangars to begin civilian operations. The large Eastern Airlines Hangar (*far top right*) was the first new airline property constructed in the postwar era (1946). (Photo courtesy of the Louisiana Division, City Archives and Special Collections, New Orleans Public Library)

Interior of the original Moisant Terminal Hangar (1946).
(Photo courtesy of the Louisiana Division, City Archives
and Special Collections, New Orleans Public Library)

domestic air service across the southern United States stretching from Florida to Southern California. New Orleans, a major city and fuel stop along the route, attracted new service from several carriers catering to coast-to-coast travelers. Soon thereafter, Delta and National Airlines opened telephone reservation centers in the city.

Since Moisant's 1946 opening as a civilian airport, Central American routes operated by Aviateca, SHASA, TACA, LACSA, and Pan American Airways dominated international service. In May 1964, Delta and Pan American Airlines provided the first joint European service to Paris and London. Delta crews flew the aircraft within the United States while Pan American crews operated the transatlantic service to Paris and London. That same year, jetways were added to the gates, providing all-indoor comfort to boarding passengers for the first time.

In 1978, National Airlines briefly introduced a nonstop flight to Amsterdam using DC-10 jumbo jet aircraft. In 1982, British Airways became the first European airline to offer scheduled flights from New Orleans with service to London originating in Mexico City, boarding passengers at New Orleans International and then continuing nonstop to the United Kingdom.

A major expansion completed in 1975, introduced two additional concourses (A and B) just in time for post deregulation expansion. One by one, beginning in 1978, Allegheny (today's US Airways), Ozark, Piedmont, and TWA, among others, added New Orleans to their "deregulation" route maps. American Airlines also reinstated scheduled service to New Orleans at this time, after a forty-five-year absence following the 1934 U.S. Airmail scandals. New Orleans International was the first airport served by Southwest Airlines outside its home state of Texas. In 1982, Senator Russell Long convinced President Ronald Reagan to amend restrictions on flights into Washington National Airport (DCA), allowing Eastern Airlines to operate nonstop service between the nation's capital and New Orleans.

Throughout the 1980s, New Orleans International was a significant battlefield within a much larger national fare war. Texas Air Corporation, parent company of Continental, had recently acquired Eastern, Frontier, New York Air, and People Express. The corporation aggressively fought to oust American, Delta, Muse Air, Southwest, and TranStar Airlines from several southern markets. Texas Air positioned flights for every brand of passenger, business and leisure, attempting to eliminate the competition through a scorched-earth policy of over-

Moisant's original wooden military air traffic control cabin was used from 1945 until the first phase of the new terminal, the North Pier (Concourse C), was completed. (Photo courtesy of the Louisiana Division, City Archives and Special Collections, New Orleans Public Library)

serving the market and underpricing the fares. Between these airlines, one-way flights to Houston costing as little as nine dollars departed New Orleans every thirty minutes during peak flying hours.

During this period, small regional airlines such as Air New Orleans, Royale, and TranStar Skylink found renewed success supporting the New Orleans battlefront by delivering passengers from Baton Rouge, Shreveport, Monroe, Alexandria, Lafayette, and Lake Charles to each of these airlines with small nineteen- to twenty-five-seat commuter planes. By 1990, the pace had slowed, and newcomers intercepted the Louisiana regional market. L'Express Airlines, a New Orleans–based commuter airline with aircraft painted in Mardi Gras colors, experienced moderate success flying as an independent intrastate airline. This hometown touch was brief. Lacking sufficient financial backing, the end for L'Express came when Florida Gulf Airways—a USAir Express affiliate supported by the strength of its major East Coast code-sharing partner, USAir, which operated larger 150-seat jet aircraft through New Orleans—seized the opportunity and overtook this small commuter market throughout the next decade.

"MSY" remains the largest and busiest commercial airport in the state, supporting, by some estimates, nearly half of south Louisiana's total population. To this day, airlines continuously devise new ways to incorporate the volatile New Orleans market into their route systems, thus enabling Louisiana residents to enjoy a variety of low-fare and major air carrier services. For instance, when new service is introduced, major airlines are forced to respond by matching a percentage of the low fares, an added boost to local business and tourism.

Recent efforts have been made to incorporate the culture of the city and the south Louisiana region into the features of the airport terminal interior. Airport vendors introducing visitors to the city emphasize artwork, specialty gift shopping, and regional meals. One of the most significant initiatives was changing the airport's name from Moisant to Louis Armstrong International Airport, executed in 2001 in coordination with a yearlong celebration of Satchmo's one-hundredth birthday.

The last remaining building from the earliest days of the airport's operation, commonly known as the TACA Air Cargo Hangar, was damaged beyond practical repair by Hurricane Katrina. As a result, the hangar and its accompanying set of military Quonset huts were demolished. Ironically, the building's final service after the storm was providing support to U.S. Army and National Guard troops evacuating New Orleans residents from the hurricane's floodwaters.

Left, Passengers arriving on an Eastern Airlines Constellation enter the original MSY terminal in early 1950. "Connies" were the premier postwar, pre–jet era transport, and Eastern served New Orleans with them from 1946 to the mid-1960s.

Below, Construction of MSY's first permanent air terminal began in early 1957. (Photos courtesy of the Louisiana Division, City Archives and Special Collections, New Orleans Public Library)

Right, The Parabola interior in 1959. (Photo courtesy of the Louisiana Division, City Archives and Special Collections, New Orleans Public Library)

Below, This 2010 photo demonstrates how the Parabola interior has evolved with the changing demands of air travel, from a 1960s spacious, contemporary lounge to a security queue in the post-911 era. (Photo by the author)

The landmark Parabola, the last section of the new terminal to be completed, was opened in 1959. (Photo courtesy of the Louisiana Division, City Archives and Special Collections, New Orleans Public Library)

Above, This 1959 pre-opening photograph shows the extended ticketing lobby, which led to an oversized picture window overlooking activity on the runway.

Right, The primary restaurant shown here in 1959, named the International Room, offered formal dining overlooking aircraft on the North Pier. (Photos courtesy of the Louisiana Division, City Archives and Special Collections, New Orleans Public Library)

In 1960, the original "Moisant" ticketing hangar (*top center*) was dwarfed by the expansive New Orleans International terminal building and its North and West boarding piers. The "terminal hangar" and original control tower (*far left*) were soon removed to make room for additional aircraft ramp space. Prior to its demolition in 1973, the original Eastern Airlines hangar (*right*) was a local Airline Highway landmark. (Photo courtesy of the Louisiana Division, City Archives and Special Collections, New Orleans Public Library)

Above, Under the new control tower on the North Pier in 1958, international carrier Aviateca operates a C-46 cargo aircraft beside an Eastern Airlines Electra preparing for boarding. (Photo courtesy of the Louisiana Division, City Archives and Special Collections, New Orleans Public Library)

Above right, On April 10, 1960, New Orleans mayor DeLesseps Morrison welcomed the first commercial jet, an Eastern DC-8, to New Orleans International, celebrating the first scheduled jet passenger service in Louisiana. (Photo courtesy of the Louisiana Division, City Archives and Special Collections, New Orleans Public Library)

Right, By the early 1960s, jets were commonplace at MSY. (Photo courtesy of the Louisiana Division, City Archives and Special Collections, New Orleans Public Library)

Opposite, Today, only a few remnants of the original 1959 terminal, now surrounded by contemporary improvements, are visible to arriving passengers. (Photo by the author)

WHAT DOES MSY STAND FOR?

New Orleans International Airport has one of the most unique three-letter aeronautical identifier codes (MSY) in the entire global air-traffic system. Its origin, which at the time of dedication was a very appropriate choice for attracting worldwide appreciation for the new facility, has long since faded from Louisiana lore. However, it remains instantaneously memorable to generations of curious travelers, pilots, and navigators flying into south Louisiana due to its "apparent" lack of connection to the destination it represents.

Although the city leaders did not have time to formally dedicate the airfield prior to the Japanese attack on Pearl Harbor and its subsequent lease by the U.S. Army Air Corps, several possible names for the new airport were suggested. The most popular honored local flyers like the Wedell brothers or Harry P. Williams. Also suggested was John Bevins Moisant, whose visit in December 1910, in spite of its tragic end, irreversibly associated the heroics of the Wright Brothers'

era of flying with the city of New Orleans. Among those residents old enough to have witnessed Moisant's performances was the wartime mayor of New Orleans, Robert Maestri.

Mayor Maestri and the New Orleans City Council considered naming the airport in honor of a hometown flyer, but options avoiding confusion with other state facilities were narrowly limited. Consensus settled upon uniqueness, in a reverent reference that would direct attention to one of the city's most famous aerial tourists— Moisant International Airport.

Once Moisant's name was chosen, a three-letter aeronautical identifier had to be put in place, a requisite for all airports operating in the United States. To fulfill the need, the initial *M*, representing Moisant's name, was added to *SY* in lighthearted recognition of the property's prior use as a prewar dairy and cattle stockyard. Thus the code *MSY* was born.

TACA—TRANSPORTES AEREOS CENTRO-AMERICANOS (CENTRAL AMERICAN AIR TRANSPORT)

New Orleans International Airport has played a pivotal role in the development of Central American air service. The airlines serving these neighboring nations, notably TACA Airlines, have also offered substantial service and support to Louisiana residents. TACA's founding within the nation of Honduras in 1931 by the New Zealand–born, American-educated investor Lowell Yerex influenced the development of routes throughout Central and South America to the point that major airlines serving the region were obligated to follow its lead. So volatile was TACA's potential that Howard Hughes, owner of TWA, was, for a time, a major stockholder in the company. This seemingly harmless airline became Hughes's weapon of choice in a Latin American business battlefront, being one of the few companies positioned to threaten the dominance of the region by Hughes's archrival, Juan Trippe.

Frequently reorganized to the taste of speculative entrepreneurs, by midcentury TACA provided cargo, passenger, and for-hire service to more than two hundred locations in the Western Hemisphere. In 1949, Waterman Steamship Company purchased the airline, and two years later formed TACA Corporation in New Orleans, where the air-

line's offices relocated to, among other facilities, a hangar and surplus military Quonset huts at Moisant International Airport.

Waterman went to great lengths to restructure the airline's network, establishing in New Orleans a pilot base, aircraft maintenance and cargo facilities, and a reservations center. El Salvador became the airline's hub, supporting daily flights operating between New Orleans, Tegucigalpa, Honduras, and other points in Central America. At its peak, TACA operated with nearly three hundred employees in the New Orleans area, with ticketing offices throughout the United States reporting to the Louisiana base. Waterman Steamship eventually sold all of its interest in the company to its stockholders and new investors, one of whom, Ricardo Kriete, took complete control of the company in 1961. Expanded service to other markets in the United States eventually included Dallas, Houston, Los Angeles, New York, Washington, D.C., and Miami.

Success gave birth to many challenges. Over time, the TACA brand evolved into a parent company, "Grupo TACA," that acquired under its wing several notable Central American airlines including Aviateca of Guatemala, Lacsa of Costa Rica, and NICA of Nicaragua. Over the years of operation at New Orleans International, disagreements between the employee unions and managers surfaced with increasing frequency, impacting the airline's growing departments. Company executives slowly relocated the infrastructure back to El Salvador. Local employees were offered the options of early retirement or relocation to the operation in El Salvador with renegotiated salaries.

Although the primary offices in New Orleans closed, TACA continued to serve the city, adjusting its schedules to meet varying demand. The final blow came when natural disasters and significant downturns in global airline industry economics caused several carriers including TACA to rework their route maps and drop service to a number of large cities. Following a year of deliberation after Hurricane Katrina, TACA elected not to reinstate its service to New Orleans, ending over a half century of continuous service to the Crescent City.

Above, TACA provided early passenger jet service between Central America and New Orleans with the British BAC 111 airliner.

Left, For nearly a half century, TACA operated international cargo flights from New Orleans with a variety of aircraft including this Canadair CL-44.

Opposite, TACA's administration was humble in budget and overhead costs. The airline operated DC-3s from former military Quonset huts and an accompanying hangar. (Photos courtesy of Mr. Peter Messina)

The original Baton Rouge Airport, shown here from the air with crowds celebrating the new terminal and hangar. These facilities continued to serve the state capital following World War II and were operational for nearly a half century (1931). (Photo courtesy of the East Baton Rouge Parish Library)

The East Baton Rouge/Downtown and Harding/Ryan Airports— Baton Rouge

In June 1931, years after attempts to fly airmail between New Orleans and Baton Rouge, Louisiana's capital opened its first public airport near the crossroads of Lobdell Avenue and Government Street. The site had been a remote open field informally used for airmail and general aviation flights supporting the oil and banking industries. A public dedication ceremony attracting thousands began on June 17 and continued through the weekend, when the airport hosted the Baton Rouge Air Races. Participants included Jimmie and Walter Wedell. Their winning trophy from the event is on display at the Louisiana State Museum in Patterson.

Early commercial flights were operated from the site by American Airways and Eastern Airlines, though American withdrew service prior to the 1934 airmail scandals. The airport is the site where, in 1936, Harry P. Williams and Wedell-Williams chief pilot Doug Worthen lost their lives when Williams's personal aircraft, a Beechcraft Staggerwing, crashed immediately after takeoff. That same year following the accident, Eastern Airlines withdrew from the airport, leaving Baton Rouge without commercial air service.

Standard Oil operated regularly out of the Baton Rouge field in association with their refinery, transporting employees to locations such as the Tallulah Airport in north Louisiana.

The need for a new airport began to be felt in the late 1930s, when larger commercial airliners appeared more frequently on Louisiana routes. The Lobdell Avenue property developed a reputation for being too small to safely accommodate the larger aircraft. As a result, in 1939 the airfield destined to become Harding Airport, later renamed Ryan Field, brainchild of the Baton Rouge Police Jury, was planned within miles of the Louisiana State Capitol Building. Development and funding for the new airport was arranged through the CAA and WPA, which paid for clearing of the land and initial construction.

The airport's military legacy began in 1940, when prior to completion as a commercial airport, the U.S. Army Air Corps leased the property from the parish. It was formally named Harding Field in 1942 in honor of Air Corps pilot William Wadley Harding, a Shreveport native who died in a training accident.

Commercial air traffic returned to Baton Rouge in 1943, when Delta Airlines extended its routes connecting north Louisiana through Alexandria and Baton Rouge into New Orleans. Eastern Airlines also

Top, Passenger and airmail operations were conducted by American Airways in the early 1930s at the original Baton Rouge terminal building and hangar. (Photo courtesy of the East Baton Rouge Parish Library)

Bottom, Today, the original hangar houses the BRCC indoor tennis courts. It is the only remaining airport structure on the property. (Photo by the author)

Right, Throughout the 1960s, Southern Airways Convair 440 aircraft were a common sight at the Ryan Passenger Terminal. (Photo courtesy of the Louisiana State Library)

Below, The new Baton Rouge terminal features a large bay window for viewing departing and arriving aircraft (2010). (Photo courtesy of the Baton Rouge Metropolitan Airport)

returned to support troop movement. A temporary terminal building was constructed on the east side of the base and operated so that it would not interfere with the military activity on the field. General aviation activity continued to operate out of the Lobdell Avenue field.

Harding Air Field was deactivated by the Air Corps in March 1945, just prior to the end of the war. The airline operations moved to the west side of the airport, which had more room for expansion and a permanent terminal building. In 1954, the airport was renamed for William Ryan, a Baton Rouge native and World War II pilot then serving on the airport board. In 1981, following additional renovation, it was again renamed the Baton Rouge Metropolitan Airport.

Baton Rouge Metropolitan Airport (BTR) has evolved into one of the busiest regional commercial airports in the state, serving residents in communities between Lafayette and New Orleans. It is home to a major maintenance facility operated by Atlantic Southeast Airlines

(ASA). ASA provides regional airline service to both Delta and United Airlines. Today, the facility provides line maintenance and major overhaul work for ASA's fleet of Canadair and Embraer regional jet aircraft. BTR also hosts one of Louisiana's most thriving general aviation infrastructures, which supports the state's government, corporations, and small businesses located in and around the capital city.

When the airfield on Lobdell Avenue closed, all remaining general aviation traffic relocated to Ryan Airport. The original terminal building has been demolished. Today the property is home to Independence Park, operated by the Recreation and Park Commission for the Parish of East Baton Rouge (BREC), the Louisiana State Police Headquarters, and the Governor's Office of Homeland Security and Emergency Preparedness (GOHSEP). The only remaining aviation structure to survive, one of the original 1931 hangars last used by Louisiana Aircraft Inc., now houses BREC's indoor tennis courts.

Above, Louisiana's capital city supports a large general and business aviation infrastructure (2010).

Left, An American Eagle Embraer 145 Regional Jet at a Baton Rouge Airport gate (2010). (Photos by the author)

Throughout World War II, the U.S. Naval Base in Houma was a primary facility for lighter-than-air operations for the entire Gulf Coast. (Photo courtesy of the Houma-Terrebonne Airport Commission)

Houma-Terrebonne Airport

From the onset of the petroleum industry's settlement in Louisiana at the beginning of the twentieth century, transportation through the bayous and wetlands of the state has been an endlessly challenging proposition. Logistics in shallow waters are as demanding as those required in deeper water or in openwater drilling, where larger vessels are able to navigate more freely.

By the 1950s, the petrochemical companies were enormously successful in prospecting and drilling and were increasing their operations in south Louisiana. Whether drilling farther offshore or closer inland, time—the crucial factor in both operations—was being lost through water travel and demanded more effective management. As operations expanded, crew boats and other swift utility vessels were stretched to their limits.

Oil companies and the multitude of smaller businesses supporting exploration and development relied heavily on aviation to transport small groups of workers and equipment to remote locations. The Houma-Terrebonne Airport is representative of several airfields in south Louisiana that fulfilled a critical mission in supporting such operations.

Construction began in the late 1920s on a site selected by Terrebonne Parish executives near Bayou Terrebonne, just outside of the city of Houma. Civilian operations catering to oil company managers and personnel traveling to nearby fields were the primary flight activity. Like other municipal airports, Houma-Terrebonne was incorporated into the War Department's operation at the outbreak of World War II. The U.S. Navy established a lighter-than-air base to patrol the Gulf Coast for enemy submarines preying on Mississippi River shipping. Runways provided access to aircraft like PBY Catalina amphibious planes supporting the base operations. Large contingents of military personnel were assigned to the airfield. The base was returned to the parish at the end of the war.

The postwar petrochemical industry boom continued to expand, supported in no small part by south Louisiana seaplane operators. At its peak, between 1950 and 1970, more than three hundred amphibious aircraft in the area provided on-demand flights, their direct service and speed often surpassing the practicality of the crew boat for transporting workers and supplies offshore.

Charles Hammonds founded his air service in Houma to support the oil industry with seaplane transportation for material and personnel to inland and offshore sites. (Photo courtesy of Charles Hammonds)

One of the most successful of these operations was Charlie Hammonds Flying Service based at the Houma-Terrebonne Airport. The company operated nine seaplanes throughout south Louisiana. In addition, Hammonds founded his own land-based scheduled airline in 1970, Hammonds Commuter Airlines, offering service from Houma to the Patterson, New Orleans, Lafayette, and Houston Hobby airports utilizing the same model aircraft as those flown by the larger commuter airlines.

Hammonds Commuter Airlines was a unique company, unlike anything in the region, operating as an FAA-registered, scheduled airline on par with operations serving larger cities. The specialty service catered to transportation of equipment sales representatives, operations managers, and the airlifting of critical parts directly to remote oil-field sites. The airline operated until 1980, when the industry revenues began to weaken. Today, larger helicopter companies have expanded their scope of operations to fill the niche originally identified by Mr. Hammonds.

Merry Christmas

and a happy new year!

Charlie Hammonds'
Flying Service

HAMMONDS COMMUTER AIRLINES

SERVING: Houston, (Hobby) TX   Houma, LA
          Lafayette, LA   New Orleans, LA
          Patterson, LA

Charter, Crew Change, and Freight
Service throughout the United States.
(up to 2000 lbs.) Seaplane service covering the entire Gulf Coast.

FAA approved maintenance.   Piper Sales & Service.
Round engines through turbines.   Approved Flight Training
South La. Avionics Center.

"COME FLY WITH US"
Hammonds has been in the flying business for more than 20 years.

Please call us for further information
Local 504 876-0584
Wats 800 535-5970 (out of state)
Wats 800 352-5989 (Louisiana)   601415   Travel Agency Computer Code: EM

Top left, In the 1970s, the flying service publicity photos were often inspired by the U.S. Navy Blue Angels aerial formations, based in Pensacola, Florida, with whom Charles Hammonds maintained a lifetime connection.

Top right, Hammonds Commuter Airlines, a branch of the company, provided service from the 1960s through the early 1980s connecting south Louisiana sites to the Gulf Coast and beyond. It was recognized as an official commuter airline by the International Air Transport Association (IATA).

Right, From charter fishing to oil field support, including during the 2010 BP oil disaster, seaplanes have played a crucial role in supporting offshore industries throughout Louisiana. (Photos courtesy of Charles Hammonds)

An aerial view of the Shreveport Downtown Airport's terminal building and hangars just prior to the relocation to SHV. (Photo courtesy of the Shreveport Airport Authority)

Shreveport was one of the postflight tour stops for Douglas "Wrong Way" Corrigan following his famous 1938 copy-cat flight of Lindbergh's Atlantic crossing. Denied permission to make the crossing, Corrigan filed a flight plan to Los Angeles but said he landed in Ireland twenty-eight hours later after getting lost in a fog. (Photo courtesy of the Shreveport Airport Authority)

Shreveport Regional and Downtown Airports

The airports operated by the City of Shreveport serve a large demographic within Louisiana, Texas, and Arkansas. The facility known today as Shreveport's Downtown Municipal Airport was constructed in 1929, with the same $1.8 million bond revenues authorized for funding of the Barksdale Army Air Base. The airfields are in close proximity to one another by design. City leaders wanted to ensure that future expansion of aviation operations could be accommodated on the adjacent property.

Left, Trans-Texas Airlines, Delta C&S, and Braniff were among the airlines serving the New Shreveport Airport after the relocation. (Photo courtesy of the Shreveport Airport Authority)

Below, Designed to accommodate ongoing expansion, today Shreveport's modern all-glass regional airline terminal is one of the most contemporary designs in the nation. (Photo courtesy of the Shreveport Airport Authority)

When the airport was completed on July 14, 1931, it was described as "little more than an open, cleared field with a windsock." It served as the primary civilian airport through World War II and was a remote landing field for nearby Barksdale training exercises. During this period, it received a number of upgrades, including paved aircraft aprons, runways, and lighting.

Today, the Downtown Airport is a designated general aviation reliever field for the city. The field is fully equipped with private hangars built to support business, corporate, and general aviation activity. The original airline terminal building was replaced with a more contemporary structure that is still in use for general aviation functions. The Downtown Airport is also home to Southern University's Aviation Airframe and Powerplant Certification Program.

The airport operated as an uncontrolled facility until February 1974, when the FAA constructed a permanent air traffic control tower on the airfield. Ironically, when the original tower was replaced with a more modern control cabin in 1981, the air traffic controllers' strike caused the tower to be closed. It would not reopen for another two years.

Immediately following World War II, it became apparent that the Shreveport/Bossier City community would require a larger airport to support increases in commercial airline traffic. City officials selected a site on the western edge of the metropolitan area approximately ten miles from the original airport to construct the new facility. The Greater Shreveport Municipal Airport, now renamed the Shreveport Regional Airport, was opened to the public on July 6, 1952. At that time, the three commercial airlines serving the city—Delta, Chicago and Southern, and Mid-Continent Airlines—transferred their operations to the new field.

A new terminal building was completed in 1998 offering increased space for support of airline operations and public amenities. The airport features AeroPark, commercial acreage set aside on airport property for development by industries and manufacturers that benefit from ready access to air transportation. One of the first new AeroPark tenants was Rockwell International, which moved an aircraft modification facility into a new hangar constructed on the site. The property was later used by Boeing, which purchased a large portion of the Rockwell International operation. Following Boeing, ExpressJet Airlines—a regional partner of Continental and United Airlines—leased the property and used it as a maintenance base for its fleet of regional and corporate jet airliners. In addition to its scheduled service, Shreveport is also home to a large fleet of general and business aviation aircraft supporting the economy of north Louisiana.

Lafayette Regional Airport

The field that is today known as Lafayette Regional Airport began supporting aircraft in the early 1930s. It operated as a remote site for over a decade with a simple infrastructure of a single hangar on an open field, allowing pilots to take off and land in any direction based on wind conditions. Outlined runways were soon added based on south Louisiana prevailing winds.

The airport was transferred from civilian operation to the U.S. Army Air Corps in July 1942 and used as a military training base. The training was executed by a locally operated civilian company, the Lafayette School of Aeronautics, under the command of the Army Air Force Gulf Coast Training Center, a branch of the U.S. Army Air Corps. The company used Fairchild PT-19, PT-17 Stearman aircraft to fulfill the mission. The base was also home to a handful of active Curtiss

P-40 Warhawk aircraft used for advanced training. Operations were closely aligned with the DeRidder and Esler Army air bases, providing cross-country flight training for pilots preparing to go overseas.

The airfield was deactivated in September 1945 and returned to the City of Lafayette for use as a civilian airport. Postwar general aviation activity supporting southeastern Louisiana petrochemical industries grew steadily. Locally owned fixed-base operators such as the Fornet Air Service supported the airport operations. The first commercial air service to Lafayette was initiated in 1948 by Eastern Airlines.

Lafayette Regional Airport's strategic geographic location makes it a focal point of Gulf Coast helicopter operations. Today, the airport is home to among other operations, the corporate headquarters of PHI, Inc., one of the largest rotary-wing air service providers in the world, as well as Air Med, the air service branch of Acadian Companies, parent of the Acadian Ambulance Service.

Top left, Operating on-demand charter for the petrochemical companies, Louisiana-based helicopters are the airlines of the industry, transporting employees and materials to rigs and other remote field sites (2010). (Photo by the author)

Above, The first contemporary Lafayette Air Terminal was a product of mid-1950s design. (Photo courtesy of the Louisiana State Library)

Left, Lafayette's new passenger terminal features a second-floor boarding lounge adorned with contemporary artwork (2010). (Photo by the author)

Opposite, The original Paul Fornet Air Service FBO, a staple of postwar aviation in Lafayette and, for that matter, the entire state of Louisiana, utilized these former World War II training hangars (2010). (Photo by the author)

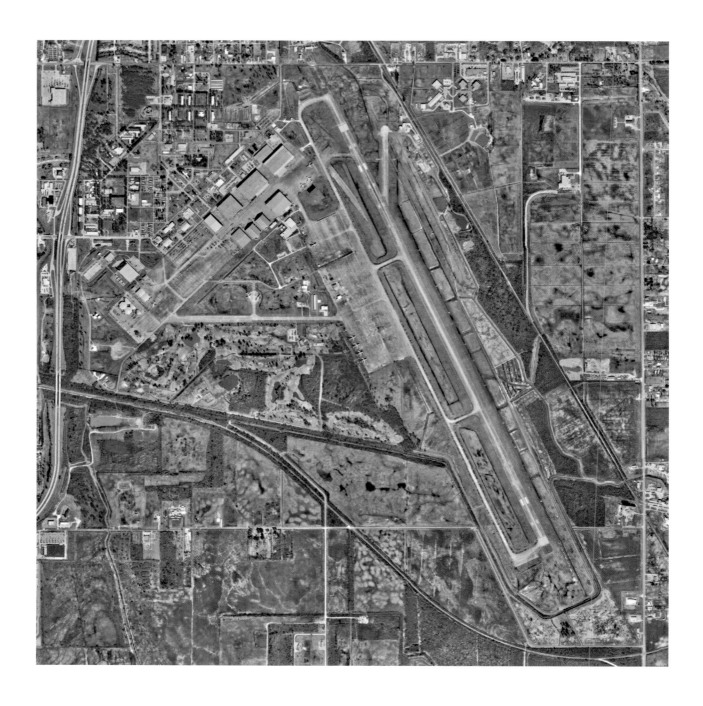

Louisiana is home to former Cold War military airfields that have successfully transitioned to viable civilian facilities following the thawing of relations with Eastern Europe. Two of the most prominent examples are the England Air Park in Alexandria and the Chennault International Airport in Lake Charles. Numerous commercial airlines use Chennault International Airport for heavy maintenance of their fleets, while England Air Park supports a number of large government aircraft.

The postmilitary potential of these airfields as engines for local economies has long been recognized. The communities of central and southwestern Louisiana have become national benchmarks for the successful transition of airports from military to civilian facilities.

Chennault International Airport—Lake Charles

Lake Charles played an influential role in preparing military aviators for combat during World War II and the Cold War. The metropolitan area is home to two airports, Chennault International and Lake Charles Regional.

Chennault's impressive aviation support complex began life as a U.S. Army Air Corps training base. In late 1941, the military leased 1,000 acres from the Calcasieu Police Jury for construction of the airfield. Opened as the Advanced Single Engine School at Lake Charles, Louisiana, the facilities supported training operations for a continuous stream of student and advanced pilots. Once the United States entered the war, the airfield was renamed the Lake Charles Army Air Field.

The facility had a sizable gunnery range for pilots to learn strafing tactics. Through the course of the war, the primary flight schools were consolidated with other bases across the country and Lake Charles was modified to accommodate additional advanced training disciplines. The base also supported medium and heavy bomber squadrons including aircraft such as the B-17, B-24, B-25, B-26, and B-29.

After the surrender of the Axis powers, Lake Charles was used to support the task of discharging countless Louisiana veterans back into civilian life. The base was decommissioned in 1946, but the outbreak of the Korean War led to its reopening in 1951. Following additional investment by the Department of Defense, it was rededicated in November 1958 as Chennault Air Force Base, in honor of Louisiana native General Claire Chennault, founder of the famous Flying Tigers American Volunteer Group, who had passed away in July of that year.

Top, Heavy strategic bombers line the aircraft aprons in the 1960s, when Chennault International was operating as Chennault Air Force Base.

Bottom, An Air Jamaica Airbus A-340 airliner being serviced at Chennault (2004).

Opposite, At 10,701 feet in length, this former military runway at Chennault International is now the longest civilian landing facility in the state (2010). (Photos courtesy of the Chennault International Airport Authority)

Top, This Ural Airlines Airbus A320, based in Yekaterinburg, Russia, underwent painting and refurbishment at Chennault International (2010). (Photo by the author)

Bottom, KC-135 military aircraft underwent complete overhaul at Chennault. Each hangar can shelter up to four of these large aircraft (2004). (Photo courtesy of the Chennault International Airport Authority)

Chennault Air Base played a vital role during the Cuban Missile Crisis and Caribbean blockade in October 1961, serving as a base of operations for long-range bombers and surveillance aircraft throughout the crisis. However, a series of military-base consolidations after the crisis led to Chennault being decommissioned a second time in 1963.

Following the closure, the Calcasieu Police Jury repurchased the base from the General Services Administration (GSA) and revitalized the land by offering long-term leases to civilian and municipal agencies. Through the years, the property has been occupied by a variety of tenants.

The parish recently developed the facilities, adding attractive amenities such as a golf course and recreation complex. SOWELA Technical Community College, a respected aircraft maintenance school provides training for students throughout southwest Louisiana. In 1986, the property was placed under the administration of its own governing authority to manage development.

Today numerous airlines and aircraft-leasing companies, many of which are international and serve neither Louisiana nor any U.S. cities, utilize Chennault International as a primary maintenance facility for major overhaul, painting, and refurbishment of their aircraft. These aircraft are flown to Chennault from airports around the world and trusted to the hands of Louisiana professionals. Northrop Grumman operates a large military aircraft overhaul facility on Chennault. Among its many contracts, one of the more visible is refurbishment of the U.S. Air Force aerial refueling tanker fleet. Aeroframe Corporation, also located on Chennault, is a major contractor servicing large commercial and military aircraft. The company has earned a global reputation for excellence in maintenance on both Airbus and Boeing jets. Aeroframe hosts hundreds of jobs for the greater Lake Charles area. These large operations, in turn, create business opportunities for smaller companies throughout the local economy, ranging from specialty tooling to other provisional support. NASA astronauts based at Houston's Ellington Air Force Base frequently use the airport for pilot training.

Not far from and complementing Chennault, Lake Charles Regional Airport (LCH) supports commercial airlines as well as general aviation operations serving the city. A recently constructed terminal building at Lake Charles Regional replaced the original terminal built in the 1950s. Contemporary in style, the new terminal features a charming southern design, complete with plantation-style columns, patios, and decorative brick walkways leading passengers into the departure and arrival area.

Within miles of Chennault International, Lake Charles Regional Airport provides commercial airline service to southwest Louisiana featuring a contemporary passenger terminal building reflecting the heritage of the region (2010). (Photo by the author)

CLAIRE LEE CHENNAULT

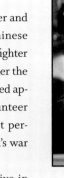

Prior to founding the Flying Tigers American Volunteer Group in the early stages of World War II, General Claire Chennault aggressively endorsed the Wedell-Williams Model 45 aircraft as an ideal pursuit plane for the U.S. Army Air Corps. Chennault grew up in Louisiana, attended LSU prior to becoming an Army pursuit pilot, and was instrumental in developing primary combat air tactics for army fighter pilots in the period between World Wars I and II.

Chennault was convinced that the 45 could satisfy the requirements of the Army's ongoing XP-34 design competition and urged Harry Williams to pursue the bid by submitting Jimmie Wedell's model. Following Jimmie Wedell's death, the Air Corps notified Williams and Chennault that the program directors had decided to cancel the original prototype and reengineer the design.

Chennault was a controversial officer with an undeserved reputation for butting heads with West Point–graduated generals (the majority of whom were not educated in aeronautics) over the operation of Air Corps squadrons. In 1937, after spending nearly thirty years on active duty, Chennault retired his commission. However, his bullish advocacy of air tactics attracted the attention of Chinese Generalissimo Chiang Kai-shek, who invited Chennault to visit China as an advisor to the Chinese air force, which was woefully inferior to the aggressive Japanese military air arm.

Chennault accepted the offer and was able to secure for the Chinese government one hundred P-40 fighter aircraft intended for Britain under the Lend Lease program. He recruited approximately two hundred volunteer pilots, mechanics, and support personnel to help Chiang Kai-shek's war effort.

Chennault's mercenaries live in history as the American Volunteer Group (AVG), more famously known as the Flying Tigers, a reference to the Louisiana Tigers Infantry Unit of the Civil War and Louisiana State University. Chennault painted a shark's mouth on the nose of each P-40 aircraft, using imagery from traditional Japanese folklore to suggest to the Japanese the presence of predators in surrounding waters.

When the United States formally entered World War II after the Japanese attack on Pearl Harbor, AVG personnel were indoctrinated into the U.S. Army Air Corps. Chennault was again commissioned into his retired rank of Army general and served the remainder of the war in the China-Burma Theater. Following this second call to duty, Chennault returned to Louisiana. He died at Oschner Foundation Hospital on Jefferson Highway in New Orleans in 1958 and is buried at Arlington National Cemetery in Washington, D.C.

The Flying Tigers have become one of the most famous fighting units in aviation history. Countless artists and combat units around the world have reproduced the famous shark's-mouth aircraft nose art.

Above, Retired General Claire Lee Chennault founded the American Volunteer Group (AVG), better known as the Flying Tigers, who challenged Japanese aggression in China during the earliest years of World War II. (Photo courtesy of Nell Calloway, Chennault Aviation and Military Museum, Office of the Louisiana Secretary of State)

Left, The P-40 Flying Tigers shark's-mouth nose art became one of the most recognized symbols of U.S. military defense during and after World War II. Since the 1950s, when the restoration of "warbird" aircraft became an industry, Chennault's nose art has become a standard at air shows and for vintage aircraft collectors. (Photo by the author)

Once based at England Air Force Base, the Twenty-third Tactical Fighter Wing carried on the tradition and excellence of Chennault's original Flying Tigers (2010). (Photo by the author)

Right, The new Alexandria International Airport Terminal at England Airpark and Community is one of the most beautifully designed and practical regional air facilities in the nation (2010).

Below, Doric columns are a feature of the terminal (2010). (Photos by the author)

Alexandria International Airport at England Air Park—Alexandria

The history of England Air Park begins in 1939, in close conjunction with Esler Army Airfield in Pineville, when the pair, operated by the U.S. Army Air Corps, supported bomber and fighter crews. The onset of World War II resulted in substantial growth in facility infrastructure. The base was renamed England Air Force Base in June 1955 for John B. England, its former commander.

Over time, the field has been home to a number of Air Force squadrons, including Cold War–era fighter and attack wings supporting tactical operations across the globe. A memorial park featuring static display of five of the former aircraft types based there welcomes visitors to the facility.

England was decommissioned in December 1992. With no possibility of the military returning to the base, a cooperative effort between the central Louisiana community and the federal government set in motion the base's long-term transition into an industrial airpark. England offered a sizable infrastructure for community development, more than 2,200 acres and multiple buildings, many of which were in move-in condition.

The England Economic and Industrial Development District, an independent authority, was created to oversee planning and development.

One of its first actions was to relocate commercial flights to Alexandria International Airport from Esler Field, now headquarters for the Louisiana National Guard, which had been handling the airlines since World War II. The original "Oak Wing" base golf course and former base housing areas were prepared for civilian occupation. Business and residential occupants are attracted by England's central location with easy access to resources throughout the state. In 1996, the successful transition attracted the attention of President Bill Clinton, who called it a model for future base closures.

By the late 1990s, England hosted a sizable aviation infrastructure for aircraft maintenance and commercial, general, and business aviation. The field is now a base of operations for a number of government aircraft. Other non-aviation-related businesses such as a magnet charter school, hospital, and truck-driver training center also relocated to the park. England has withstood downturns of the economy through the two decades since the base closed and is positioned to support the regional area in a unique way.

England's commercial air terminal is considered one of the finest contemporary regional facilities in the nation, impeccably landscaped and complementing the community with an exquisite exterior reflective of the Red River region. The terminal features an equally impressive spacious interior positioned for future expansion.

Flowing water at the terminal entrance reminds patrons of the Red River's historic importance to central Louisiana (2010). (Photo courtesy of the England Air Park and Community)

Caldwell Parish Library
P.O. Box 1499
Columbia, La. 71418

CHAPTER FIVE

LOUISIANA'S HOMETOWN AIRPORTS

In addition to the airports supporting commercial airline operations, an abundance of smaller general aviation airports thrive throughout the state. These airports have an unmistakable hometown feel, supported by regional municipalities and the passion of local aviators.

While several of these airports were developed from smaller outlying support military training fields, most of these facilities were constructed through the initiatives of the individual parishes. Regardless of its origins, Louisiana's network of general aviation airports is a vital engine for local economies.

General aviation airports fill two critical roles. First, each uniquely supports its parish or municipality by providing a venue for air taxi service and charter flights for individuals, businesses, and emergency medical transportation. Specialty businesses such as crop-dusting companies are also based at local community airports. Second, airports provide communities with recreational resources ranging from flight instruction and weekend pleasure flying to educational programs that introduce the general public to the behind-the-scenes support that local airports provide to their communities.

Agricultural pilots check wind and drift over target fields by releasing a smoke trail prior to disbursement of fertilizers and insecticides (2010). (Photo by the author)

CROP-DUSTING

One of Louisiana's most significant contributions to aviation was the invention of aerial crop-dusting. The concept of applying pesticides and fertilizers to large areas of farmland by air rather than through the hazardous manual labor of hundreds of field hands on the ground was a direct result of the work of entomologists Dr. B. R. Coad, director of the Louisiana branch of the U.S. Department of Agriculture, and his assistant C. E. Woolman (see chapter 2). Now practiced regularly, this innovative approach to defending agriculture from insects grew from an experiment supporting north Louisiana farmers into a standard global procedure.

Dr. Coad founded the "Delta Lab" in Tallulah, Louisiana, to accurately measure the impact of pests on area farms. The study progressed rapidly when Woolman incorporated aerial spraying into the research program, identifying multiple methods of releasing pesticides by air.

Having no aircraft of their own at the time, Dr. Coad and Woolman enlisted the U.S. Army Air Corps for aerial support. Through a series of experiments and test flights, the earliest aircraft used for crop-dusting were modified Air Corps training planes capable of carrying little more than the weight of the chemicals to be applied. Later aircraft offered more powerful engines with greater horsepower, a key resource for agricultural pilots. Following World War II, the abundance of surplus aircraft, especially the versatile Stearman trainers used by the U.S. Navy and U.S. Army Air Corps, once again revolutionized the operation by increasing frequency and capacity to serve farmers.

Much like the Stearman, 1950s-era custom agricultural aircraft often featured a double "bi-wing" structure used by numerous spraying companies. These aircraft operated well into the 1970s. Casual observers have been known to mistake these crop-dusters for older World War I–era aircraft. Dusting airplanes have evolved considerably in the twentieth century, and modern fleets of today feature a more contemporary appearance.

Crop-dusting operations take place in many rural areas throughout the state, ranging from sugarcane and rice farms in the south to cotton and soybean fields in the north. Operating aircraft can be observed in flight throughout the agricultural season, peaking approximately six months out of the year between late spring and early winter. The majority of dusting companies are small, often single-owner operations that contract to multiple farmers in specific geographic regions.

Top, A Natchitoches-based duster takes off on its mission (2010).

Bottom, Passes are executed at or below treetop level, demanding exceptional piloting skill (2010). (Photos by the author)

Quick ground turns are orchestrated by awaiting refillers. With their aircraft engines idled and props "feathered," pilots do not leave the cockpits and are airborne again within minutes (2010).

When dusting season is at its peak, fleets of dusters stand by for refilling (2010). (Photos by the author)

The aircraft are centrally based at smaller airports located within the spraying areas. Municipal airports such as Natchitoches, Houma-Terrebonne, Columbia, and Tallulah, to name only a few, are home to these flight operations. Some larger operators with multiple planes may relocate their aircraft and conduct spraying outside of local regions to accommodate additional customers.

Agricultural engineers have refined the techniques that Woolman and Dr. Coad created. These modern innovations offer several possibilities for applying chemicals over a wide area. For instance, depending on the needs of the farmer, attachments under the wing of the aircraft could release a wide spray of pesticides and fertilizers, as well as a narrower, strategically targeted application of any number of products delivered through release mechanisms under the fuselage.

Such technical advances in dusting especially after the Second World War were beneficial not only to Louisiana farmers but to agricultural interests throughout the United States. Accompanying increased spraying was the potential for unforeseen hazards such as accidental chemical runoff. Today the threat is minimal and easily contained. Member associations such as the National Agricultural Aviation Association maintain professional operating standards. The U.S. Department of Agriculture and the Environmental Protection Agency, which actively monitor dusting operations and enforce regulatory compliance, regulate procedures such as aircraft loading and the mixing and release of chemicals.

Pilots specializing in agricultural aviation receive highly regulated training. The aircraft operate and are licensed under an FAA "Restricted" permit, meaning that they can only be utilized for agricultural spraying. All "Ag Pilots" must have a commercial pilot's certificate and medical certificate in order to operate an aircraft of this type. Some aircraft require the pilot to obtain a type rating, which indicates the power of the aircraft and its specific purpose. Each pilot must become proficient in a number of unique flight skills, among them an above-average command of tight turns and ability to maneuver over an often unforgiving windy field. Crop-dusting pilots operate at high speeds and must be able to fly at altitudes below the treetop level for increased precision.

As a result, agricultural flying has advanced in proportion to and no differently from passenger airliners, business aviation, and other aerospace industries. Global Positioning Systems are used for precision delivery of the spray just as general aviation aircraft and commercial airliners use this equipment for navigation. Agricultural aircraft engines have evolved from piston power plants to turbo-jet-powered propeller designs. This great leap in horsepower affords the pilot additional payload, time in the air over the crop, and cost-effective use of fuel.

Contemporary turbo-prop dusters have extensive endurance. Pilots make multiple takeoffs and landings on a single tank of fuel, with time in the air limited only by the delivery of the chemicals over the target, which sometimes spans only a few minutes.

Diligence and precision. Steep turns must become second nature to ag crews. Low-level obstacles including trees, rural utility poles, and an increasing number of cell phone towers are constant hazards along the flight path (2010). (Photo by the author)

Few airports in the world can match the picturesque approach path into Pineville Municipal (2010). (Photo courtesy of Mr. Lonnie J. Lucius, IV, Flightline Air Service, Pineville Regional Airport)

Opposite left, The St. John the Baptist FBO, located on the Parish airport in Reserve in the center of Louisiana's River Road Plantations, is typical of numerous active rural operations hosted by municipalities throughout the state (2009). (Photo by the author)

Opposite right, Aircraft on the ramp at Natchitoches Regional (2010). (Photo by the author)

GENERAL AVIATION AIRPORTS

General aviation airports are located throughout small and large communities in Louisiana. To put the critical importance of general aviation fields in perspective, there are approximately seventy public airports in Louisiana, only seven of which host scheduled airline service. The majority of Louisiana's public airports were constructed to strategically support local citizens and business flyers living in communities not served by passenger airlines.

Fixed-base operators, or FBOs, as these businesses are commonly known, are the centerpiece of general aviation airports, supporting pilots and aircraft owners with everything from fuel, aircraft maintenance, day and overnight aircraft "tie-down," and supplemental services such as catering, auto rental, and hotel accommodations for passengers and crew upon arrival.

The overwhelming majority of FBOs serving general aviation nationwide are small, independent companies ranging from mom-and-pop family operations to small partnerships. FBOs supporting smaller airports are sometimes operated by the municipality itself. Those servicing larger airports usually align with global FBO franchises, attracting corporate business aviation by offering a standardized service at major general aviation airports frequented by the customer throughout the world.

An FBO in its simplest terms is thought of as a gas station for airplanes, selling aircraft fuel and providing the pilot with the ground support necessary to prepare for and complete a flight. Pilots and passengers traveling on general aviation aircraft, corporate aircraft, or aircraft operated by small to medium-sized businesses arrive and depart through the FBO waiting area rather than the airport's main commercial terminal building.

FBOs offer a local character all their own, serving aircraft owners and pilots who rent space on the airport to store their aircraft. In Louisiana, that local character is provided through one of the most unique elements of service for flight crews—catering that features Louisiana cooking as a primary attraction. General aviation pilots around the United States, even those on transcontinental trips landing only momentarily to refuel, appreciate that a stop at a Louisiana airport means incredible meals and hospitable service.

Unfortunately, in recent years, many of the mom-and-pop operations have been forced to align with larger franchises to remain in business and thus are no longer strictly local operations. Some general aviation pilots worry that the small, independently operated FBO may become a thing of the past, replaced by a sometimes impersonal, standardized industry. While such conclusions and the extent of this transition are matters of opinion, Louisiana's general aviation airports and FBO operators continue to understand the value of incorporating the state's culture into a warm reception for their customers. The majority of these operations continue to represent their home communities with unmatched local flavor. Each still extends unforgettable aerial welcomes to tourists and businesspeople alike, giving Louisiana's airport gateways a distinct advantage over those in other parts of the country vying for the same dollars and economic support.

Above, A Beechcraft Bonanza lands at the Louisiana Regional Airport in Gonzales (2010). (Photo by the author)

Right, Southern comfort, uniquely Louisiana (2010). (Photo by the author)

Opposite, The Pineville Fly-In invites local aircraft owners, visiting pilots, and aviation enthusiasts alike to enjoy the picturesque airport (2010). (Photo courtesy of Mr. Lonnie J. Lucius, IV, Flightline Air Service, Pineville Regional Airport)

FLY-INS AND AIR SHOWS

Most individuals who are passionate about flying—especially the far larger population of nonpilot enthusiasts in comparison to the number of licensed private and commercial pilots—or who simply enjoy watching airplanes take off and land, are familiar with large air shows hosted on military bases around the state. However, in addition to these large multiday presentations, there are other regularly scheduled events, more frequent and personal in nature, that offer insight into the operational value of area airports and aviation activities specific to their locale. These are the celebrations of the aerial community known as Fly-Ins.

In the spirit of Louisiana tailgating and family barbeques, Fly-Ins are weekend events hosted by airport managers and tenants. At a Fly-In, local aircraft owners and pilots welcome the general public onto the airport hangars to learn about aviation and see firsthand how aviation supports their businesses and personal lives.

Yet another objective of a Louisiana Fly-In is to entice aircraft owners throughout the southern United States to fly their personal aircraft to the host airport and spend a day, which regularly turns into a full weekend, experiencing the local regional culture and enjoying the camaraderie of other pilots and enthusiasts. The long-term benefit for the region is aerial tourism, where visitors who would ordinarily not think of visiting these communities suddenly become regular visitors, discovering new pleasures and spending money in the local shops and restaurants. For pilot and nonpilot alike, Fly-Ins afford a unique introduction to the recreational and economic value of the general aviation airports that support small communities across Louisiana.

Bottom, Natchitoches Regional Airport hosts regular events, attracting pilots and guests to its hangars by catering with its famous meat pies (2010). (Photo by the author)

Top, Louisiana participants seldom hold back their spirit at Fly-Ins (2010). (Photo courtesy of Mr. Lonnie J. Lucius, IV, Flightline Air Service, Pineville Regional Airport)

The Fly-In concept had humble beginnings, starting as small parties organized by a handful of pilots who simply wanted an excuse to fly across the state. Having grown in popularity rapidly over the past decade, they are especially valuable economically to small rural airports not regularly visited by aircraft operators from out of the area.

Sometimes Fly-Ins are organized around a single aircraft type; for instance, Cessna or Piper aircraft operators might be encouraged to gather and talk about their experiences. Other gatherings welcome any and all aircraft owners and visitors. Fly-Ins usually do not involve corporate displays, such as manufacturers of avionics or pilot supplies, though sales representatives occasionally "drop in" to promote products of interest to participants.

The key to getting the most out of Fly-Ins is to remember that they are distinctly local affairs. Each event proudly represents its region by featuring local meals, from the meat pies of Natchitoches to the Creole cooking of south Louisiana and the endless varieties of gumbo throughout the state. Fly-Ins promote aviation on a much more personal scale than that of large air shows. Some hosts take it one step further, putting on hangar dances in the evening following the Fly-In event, featuring old-time music and vintage aircraft standing in as ballroom props.

Fly-Ins provide a wealth of information and occasionally offer introductory flights to young adults through aviation organizations such as the "Young Eagles" program sponsored by the Experimental Aircraft Association (EAA). Such flights are outstanding opportunities for aircraft owners to share their experiences with students interested in learning to fly. The Louisiana chapters of the EAA coordinate a "Louisiana Fly-In Series" that allows all participating airports to reduce the possibility of multiple events being scheduled on a single day, thus affording the maximum exposure for Louisiana general aviation.

Numerous larger municipal general aviation airports across the state, for instance, Acadiana Regional in New Iberia and the Tallulah/Vicksburg Regional in Tallulah, host air shows similar to those on military bases to entertain and promote civilian flying. Like their larger military counterparts, these shows host precision flight teams and provide demonstrations of aviation in action. Often, air ambulance and emergency rescue operations are demonstrated in these performances, offering residents a glimpse of the complex planning that accompanies aerial life support. These shows also host static displays and flights of vintage aircraft surviving from the first one hundred years of human flight.

"Smoke On!" The Aeroshell Flight Team features Louisiana-based pilots who perform precision maneuvers at air shows throughout the United States. Here the team performs at the annual Acadiana Air Show in New Iberia. (Photo by the author)

Right, Autograph sessions by performing pilots are one of many featured events at the shows (2010).

Bottom right, Corkey Fornof assists fellow Louisiana aerobatic pilot Chuck Vincent of Lafayette at the Acadiana Regional Air Show. (Photos by the author)

Thrills for another air show audience as Chuck Vincent performs. (Photo courtesy
of the author)

Right, Many aircraft owners showcase homebuilt aircraft at the Fly-Ins across Louisiana (2010).

Bottom right, Warbirds are a staple of every ramp static display. This TBM Avenger is a regular guest at events such as the N'awlins Air Show at NAS New Orleans. (Photos by the author)

Military-base presentations such as this 1960s open house at Barksdale Air Force Base, in contrast to Fly-Ins and regional air shows, are historically larger, less personal events sometimes attracting tens of thousands of spectators throughout air show weekends. (Photo courtesy of the Louisiana Division, City Archives and Special Collections, New Orleans Public Library)

The Gravity Devils, an award-winning Louisiana-based skydiving team, at ease prior to an air show jump. *Left to right:* Jason Romero (New Iberia), Corey Soignet (Gray), Dustan Daigle (Lafayette), and Jacques E. deMoss (Lafayette) (2010). (Photo by the author)

The Aeroshell Flight Team is all smiles after a performance (2010).
(Photo by the author)

CONCLUSION

The world celebrated its first century of flight in grandeur. Aviation, progressing from its beginnings with aircraft constructed of fabric, wood, and string, has been transformed by ever-developing technology, and has allowed humans to enter the skies of the new millennium in aircraft capable of transporting five hundred passengers nonstop more than three-quarters of the way around the globe. Letters and packages that once took weeks to travel by land and water route to remote populations now complete the journey within hours, and aircraft regularly navigate across continents and oceans by day and overnight. Aviation has, in effect, cross-pollinated every culture and economy.

One cannot help but wonder what Jimmie and Walter Wedell, Harry P. Williams, Collett Everman Woolman, James Menefee, and their hardworking associates might have thought of these accomplishments and of the clear influence of their work that is evident in their home state of Louisiana today. The passion they brought from the swamps and farmlands of Louisiana in pursuit of speed and economy led to precedent-setting developments in aircraft operations. Louisiana residents can take pride in knowing that the early home-based aviation innovators from their state have made the earth a much more efficient domain.

The long-term impacts of these early-twentieth-century accomplishments, not the least of which are increased accessibility and improved quality of life, sometimes remain unrecognized, especially in smaller communities. Populations throughout the United States have benefitted immeasurably from the development of farmland crop-dusting and the refining of application techniques that were born in the skies of Tallulah. The modern U.S. Postal Service owes at least some of its contemporary success to the energies of persons like Merrill Riddick, who tirelessly experimented with delivering the mail over unforgiving distances. Having inspired and tested flyers past, Louisiana aviation, with its contemporary infrastructure supporting our cultural and economic growth, is positioned to expand this influence for another one hundred years.

APPENDIX

LOUISIANA'S PUBLIC AIRPORTS

FAA CODE	AIRPORT NAME	CITY	PARISH
0R3	Abbeville Chris Crusta Memorial	Abbeville	Vermilion
AEX	Alexandria International	Alexandria	Rapides
ESF	Esler Regional	Alexandria	Rapides
5F0	Arcadia/Bienville	Arcadia	Bienville
2F8	Morehouse Memorial	Bastrop	Morehouse
BTR	Baton Rouge Metropolitan	Baton Rouge	East Baton Rouge
BXA	George R. Carr Memorial	Bogalusa	Washington
2R6	Bunkie Municipal	Bunkie	Avoyelles
F86	Columbia	Columbia	Caldwell
0R7	Red River Parish	Coushatta	Red River
L31	St. Tammany Regional	Covington	St. Tammany
3R2	Legros Memorial	Crowley	Acadia
0M9	Delhi Municipal	Delhi	Richland
5R8	DeQuincy Industrial Airpark	DeQuincy	Calcasieu
DRI	Beauregard Regional	DeRidder	Beauregard
4R7	Eunice	Eunice	Acadia
F87	Farmerville	Farmerville	Union
2R7	Franklinton	Franklinton	Washington
GAO	South Lafourche	Galliano	Lafourche
L38	Louisiana Regional	Gonzales	Ascension
HDC	Hammond Northshore Regional	Hammond	Tangipahoa
5F4	Homer Municipal	Homer	Claiborne
HUM	Houma/Terrebonne	Houma	Terrebonne
2R1	LeMaire Memorial	Jeanerette	Iberia
1R1	Jena	Jena	LaSalle
3R7	Jennings	Jennings	Jefferson Davis
F88	Jonesboro	Jonesboro	Jackson
L32	Jonesville	Jonesville	Catahoula
LFT	Lafayette Regional	Lafayette	Lafayette
CWF	Chennault International	Lake Charles	Calcasieu
LCH	Lake Charles Regional	Lake Charles	Calcasieu
0M8	Byerley	LakeProvidence	East Carroll
L39	Leesville	Leesville	Vernon
3F3	C.E. Rusty Williams Memorial	Mansfield	DeSoto
3R4	Hart	Many	Sabine
MKV	Marksville Municipal	Marksville	Avoyelles
F24	Minden	Minden	Webster
MLU	Monroe Regional	Monroe	Ouachita
IER	Natchitoches Regional	Natchitoches	Natchitoches
ARA	Acadiana Regional	New Iberia	Iberia
MSY	New Orleans Downtown Heliport	New Orleans	Orleans
NEW	New Orleans Lakefront	New Orleans	Orleans
MSY	New Orleans International	New Orleans	Jefferson
HZR	False River Regional	New Roads	Pointe Coupee
9M6	Kelly	Oak Grove	West Carroll
L42	Allen Parish	Oakdale	Allen
L47	Olla	Olla	LaSalle
OPL	St. Landry Parish	Opelousas	St. Landry
PTN	Harry P. Williams Memorial	Patterson	St. Mary
2L0	Pineville	Pineville	Rapides
L66	Pollock Municipal	Pollock	Grant
M79	John H. Hooks, Jr. Memorial	Rayville	Richland
1L0	St. John the Baptist Parish	Reserve	St. John
RSN	Ruston Regional	Ruston	Lincoln

Louisiana's Public Airports (*continued*)

FAA CODE	AIRPORT NAME	CITY	PARISH
SHV	Shreveport Regional	Shreveport	Caddo
DTN	Shreveport Downtown	Shreveport	Caddo
ASD	Slidell	Slidell	St. Tammany
SPH	Springhill	Springhill	Webster
L33	Tensas Parish	St. Joseph	Tensas
UXL	Southland Field	Sulpher	Calcasieu
TVR	Vicksburg-Tallulah Regional	Tallulah	Madison
M80	Scott	Tallulah	Madison

FAA CODE	AIRPORT NAME	CITY	PARISH
L83	Thibodaux	Thibodaux	Lafourche
0R4	Concordia Parish	Vidalia	Concordia
3F4	Vivian	Vivian	Caddo
6R1	Welsh	Welsh	Jefferson Davis
0R5	David G. Joyce	Winnfield	Winn
F89	Winnsboro Municipal	Winnsboro	Franklin
1R4	Woodworth	Woodworth	Rapides

LOUISIANA'S AVIATION MUSEUMS

Throughout the state, there are numerous collections of aircraft and artifacts, military and civilian, public and private, that preserve the unique contributions that Louisiana citizens have made to aviation. Since the number of such collections is vast, an online search tailored to your individual interests is recommended. The following museums are among those that feature displays specifically related to the history of civil aviation in Louisiana:

The Wedell-Williams Memorial Aviation Museum
A branch of the Louisiana State Museum, Patterson

The Chennault Aviation and Military Museum
A branch of the Office of the Louisiana Secretary of State, Monroe

The Hermione Museum
Featuring a well-crafted historic display of crop-dusting operations in north Louisiana, Madison Parish, Tallulah

In addition, the Delta Air Transport Heritage Museum located in Atlanta, Georgia, tells the story of the airline's founding and early years in Louisiana. The museum's collection features a full-size façade of the original Delta Air Service terminal building that was located at the Monroe Regional Airport.

LOUISIANA'S COLLEGE AVIATION PROGRAMS

Nearly every public airport in the state hosts FAA-trained flight instructors who are available to assist persons interested in obtaining a private pilot's license. For individuals interested in more advanced academic studies, the following Louisiana universities offer degree programs in aviation:

Louisiana Tech University, Ruston

Louisiana Technical College, campuses statewide

Northwestern State University, Natchitoches

Southern University, Shreveport

SOWELA Technical Community College, Lake Charles

University of Louisiana, Monroe

LOUISIANA'S AVIATION ORGANIZATIONS

The Experimental Aircraft Association (EAA) is a nationwide organization dedicated to aviation education and preservation. Most impressive is its ongoing program "The Young Eagles," which offers introductory flights at reduced or, for certain events, no cost to elementary and high school students interested in aviation. Louisiana has numerous active local EAA chapters that host monthly meetings based at airports throughout the state. The organization's national website (www.eaa.org) can provide contacts for your area.

The Civil Air Patrol (CAP) also has numerous local Louisiana chapters offering membership to students and adults, and provides a complete program of aviation orientation. The CAP's primary mission is to support search-and-rescue efforts for missing aircraft and pilots (www.lawcap.org).

The Ninety-Nines, Inc, the International Organization of Women Pilots, is an organization specifically dedicated to supporting female pilots, providing camaraderie, and generating interest in aviation as both a passion and a profession. Information on Louisiana chapters and meetings can be found at www.ninety-nines.org.

Finally, there are numerous aviation clubs and events at local airports that welcome new participants. Anyone from active pilot to armchair enthusiast is invited to share in the spirit and adventure. For information on such organizations, visit a nearby general aviation airport.

LaAviator (www.LaAviator.com) is an outstanding resource for Louisiana flyers. This website, created by Jim Riviere, is a combination news and communications page specifically for Louisiana pilots and enthusiasts. The site features a regularly updated calendar noting events such as Fly-Ins, air shows, and aviation seminars throughout the state.

Above left, The Louisiana State Museum, Patterson Branch, home of the Wedell-Williams Collection (2010). (Photo by the author)

Above, Student pilots of the Wedell Williams Flight School in Patterson prepare for a day of training (1931). (Photo courtesy of the Louisiana State Museum)

The Aircraft Instrument Landing System at the Harry P. Williams Memorial Airport, Patterson (2010). (Photo by the author)

ACKNOWLEDGMENTS

The University of New Orleans Earl K. Long Library, Louisiana and Special Collections, is home to the Newman Collection, which documents early civilian aviation in the 1920s and 1930s, and the Shushan Collection, containing memorabilia from the Shushan family and documenting the airport's incredible original splendor.

The Historic New Orleans Collection (THNOC) has amassed a large collection of aviation-related photographs from every era discussed in this book. The collection extends beyond the scope of New Orleans and helps preserve all aspects of Louisiana aviation. The collection's founder, Kemper Williams, was the older brother of Wedell-Williams Air Service founder, Harry P. Williams.

Various collections of photographs, documents, and other memorabilia representing the growth of Delta Airlines have survived through the years. The Louisiana State University Hill Memorial Library is home to the C. E. Woolman Collection. It contains an interesting mix of handwritten notes from Woolman's early journals as an agent of the USDA. The journals are accompanied by annual reports generated by Delta Airlines through 1966, the year of Woolman's death. The library also features rare photos within the T. Harry Williams Oral History Collection of Harry P. Williams and Marguerite Clark.

The Louisiana State Museum is dedicated to the preservation of the Wedell-Williams legacy. The museum's Patterson branch is partnered with the Wedell-Williams Memorial Museum Foundation and has thousands of photographs and artifacts available for aviation research. Without the resources of this magnificent collection and its professional staff, this work would have been incomplete. Thanks and appreciation are extended to the museum staff at its home offices in New Orleans for arranging numerous visits and access to these collections.

The New Orleans Public Library Main Branch is a primary source for the political history of New Orleans. These well-maintained and under-appreciated archives contain, among other documents, volumes of photographs associated with New Orleans mayors DeLesseps Story "Chip" Morrison, Victor H Schiro, and Maurice "Moon" Landrieu that were used to illustrate the history of the New Orleans International Airport.

In addition, the Latter Memorial Branch of the New Orleans Public Library, located within the original home of Harry P. Williams and Marguerite Clark on St. Charles Avenue in New Orleans, provided photographs of Miss Clark taken during her acting career.

The Louisiana State Library generously allowed use of its Digital Photograph Collection containing numerous historical images of airports throughout the state from various eras within the story.

The Minnesota State Historical Society offered photographs relative to their hometown aviation hero, Charles A Lindbergh.

The Delta Air Transport Heritage Museum provided historic photographs ranging from the airline's humble beginnings in Monroe, Louisiana, to the one-of-a kind *Spirit of Delta* Boeing 767 that once flew as a living memorial to the corporation's original spirit.

One of my goals in this book has been to acknowledge the history, work, and economic impact of all Louisiana airports and the staff members throughout the state who keep our economy flying. The following facilities provided "nonstop" support in telling this story in its whole and individual parts:

Acadiana Regional Airport, New Iberia

Alexandria International Airport, England Air Park, Alexandria

Baton Rouge Metropolitan Airport, Baton Rouge

Chennault International Airport, Lake Charles

Houma-Terrebonne Municipal Airport, Houma

Lafayette Regional Airport, Lafayette

Lake Charles Regional Airport, Lake Charles

Louis Armstrong New Orleans International Airport, Kenner

Louisiana Regional Airport, Gonzales

Monroe Regional Airport, Monroe

Natchitoches Regional Airport, Natchitoches

Pineville Municipal Airport, Pineville

Shreveport Downtown Airport, Shreveport

Shreveport Regional Airport, Shreveport

St. John the Baptist Parish Regional Airport, Reserve

Harry P. Williams Memorial Airport, Calumet

I would like to give special thanks to the following persons and organizations for providing invaluable support in the research, my photography for, and the production of this work:

Aeroshell Aerobatic Team: Alan Henley—Team Lead; Mark Henley—Right Wing; Brian Regan—Team Lead; Gene McNeely—Slot; Steve Gustafson—Left Wing; Jimmy Fordham—Wing

Heath Allen, Manager, Lake Charles Regional Airport

Carolyn Bennett, Executive Director, Foundation for Historical Louisiana

Nancy Murphy Bernard, a dear classmate and friend of many years ago who provided heartwarming company while I visited the Chennault International Airport. I am convinced that the spirit of her grandfather, Mr. Ray Braud, a key employee of the Wedell-Williams Air Service, acted as a guiding force in our paths crossing again after nearly thirty years. On one particular visit to southwestern Louisiana, although I was already familiar with Mr. Braud's work, I was amazed to learn that this charming lady was his granddaughter. Thank you, Mr. Braud! Thanks, Nancy!

Judy Bolton, LSU Hill Memorial Library Special Collections

Diana Buckley, Curator of Science and Technology at the Louisiana State Museum, made several extra trips to the Patterson Museum at my request. Thanks for all the support!

Kyle Bull, Chennault International Airport

Etienne Joseph Caire II, U.S. Naval Aviator, my original aviation mentor and inspiration

Rachel Caire, for her artistic photography of Louisiana clouds

Nell Calloway, Director, Chennault Aviation and Military Museum

David Campbell, for offering images from his private airline photo collection

Gwen McKneely Carter, niece of "Bo" McKneely, for retrieving private family photographs. Thank you, Gwen, for the personal recollections that confirmed several oral histories of the courage displayed and heartache endured by this wonderful man.

James Clifford, UNO Earl K. Long Library

William Cooksey, Manager of Marketing, Shreveport Regional Airport

Larry Cooper, Manager, Natchitoches Regional Airport

Donny Crow, Head of Photographic Services, Louisiana Tech University

Jason Devillier, Manager, Acadiana Regional Airport

Lawrence and Beverly Dorsa, for being there when time was critical

Farm Air Services, Inc., Tallulah, La.

Marie Force, Delta Air Transport Heritage Museum

Corkey Fornof, for providing encouragement and stories from his career in the James Bond 007 movies and other classic motion picture industry air operations

Scott Gammel, Manager, Alexandria International Airport

Fred Gaumnitz, Tallulah, La.

John Grafton, Executive Director, England Air Park

Virginia, Elise, and Dr. Charles Grenier, for their endless encouragement and coffee. Also, a very special thanks, Dr. Grenier, for the first proofreads!

Steve Gustafson, Warbird Pilot Extraordinaire, Certified Commercial Aerial Applicator (Crop-Duster), Left Wing on the

Aeroshell Aerobatic Team, and operator of the Tallulah Airport. Thanks for helping me get together with the great folks on the North Louisiana Duster Circuit!

Daniel Hammer, Head of Reader Services at the Historic New Orleans Collection

Charlie Hammonds, for sharing incredible stories and photos (I wish I could have fit them all in!). Thanks again for the insight into the unique history of seaplane operations in south Louisiana and the Gulf of Mexico.

Gabe Harrell, LSU Hill Memorial Library, Special Collections

Ralph Hennessy, Assistant Director, Baton Rouge Metropolitan Airport

Charles Harvey, Deputy Director, Chennault International Airport

Dr. Florence Jumonville, Chair, Louisiana and Special Collections Department, University of New Orleans Earl K. Long Library. Thank you for your encouragement throughout the entire research process.

Gloria Lacoste, Acting Director, Louisiana State Museum, Wedell-Williams Memorial Museum in Patterson, for endless support during my visits

Greg Lambousy, Director of Collections, Louisiana State Museum

Desmond J. Larrousse, Louisiana State Museum, Patterson

Karen Leathem, Museum Historian, Louisiana State Museum

The staff of the Louisiana Department of Transportation and Development-Aviation Division, especially Brad Brandt, Director, and Tanya Schulingkamp, Sr. Program Manager, without whom near instantaneous contact with the numerous airport staff members throughout the state would have been far more challenging. Brad's and Tanya's continuous willingness to immediately offer assistance of any kind was irreplaceable. Last, but not least, thanks to Mr. Phil Jones, Director of DOTD's Intermodal Transportation Division

Margaret H. Lovecraft, Acquisitions Editor, Louisiana State University Press

Lonnie J. Lucius IV, Manager, Pineville Regional Airport

John Magill of The Historic New Orleans Collection

John Earl Martin of the Hermione Museum in Tallulah, La. Mr. Martin has written a very thorough history of agricultural aviation in Madison Parish that is available at the museum. In addition, thanks, John, for being my guide and chauffeur through the Tallulah farms during the dusting season.

Shelley Masog, Librarian I, Latter Branch, New Orleans Public Library

Jerry McKinney, Manager, Shreveport Downtown Airport

Tiffany Meng, Delta Air Transport Heritage Museum

Mr. Peter Messina, for generously offering photographs and reflections on his more than forty-year career with TACA Airlines in New Orleans. And special thanks to his son John Messina for arranging our visit.

Rick Moran, Manager, St. John the Baptist Parish Airport

Mrs. Beverly Murphy, for inviting me into her home and sharing an amazing dinner filled with recollections of the work of her father, Ray Braud, at the Wedell-Williams Air Service, Shushan Airport, and the old Eastern Airlines hangar at New Orleans International Airport. In addition, a special thanks to Mr. "Al" and Tim Murphy for their anecdotes during this visit.

Susan Murray, for the editing

Derrick J. Naquin, Technician, Louisiana State Museum Patterson, frankly, the "all-around get-it-done guy" who provided continuous service in addition to locating photographs and artifacts in the museum archives.

Ronaldo "Ron" Nodal Jr., Airport Operations Manager, New Orleans International Airport

Cleve Norrell, Airport Manager, Monroe Regional Airport

Doug Parker, *Times-Picayune New Orleans*

Charles Pautler, Historic Site Manager, Charles A. Lindbergh Site, Minnesota Historical Society

Andrea Pelloquin, Executive Secretary, Chennault International Airport

Jon Proctor, my friend and very first aviation editor from periodicals past, who provided several photographs from his private collection that made the story so much easier to tell.

Randy Robb, Executive Director, Chennault International Airport

Sam Rykels, Former Director, Louisiana State Museum

Elizabeth Sherwood, Assistant Registrar and Curator, Louisiana State Museum

David Slayter, Manager, Houma-Terrebonne Airport

Stephen Tynes, Airport Operations, Louis Armstrong New Orleans International Airport

Chuck Vincent, Aerobatic Pilot and CEO, Global Data Systems, Inc.

Irene Wainwright, Archivist for the New Orleans Public Library, for generous assistance with photographs of New Orleans International Airport

Anthony Ware, Director of Airport Operations, Chennault International Airport

Geneva Rountree Williams, Curator, Hermione Museum in Tallulah, for her assistance with researching photographs of aviation in north Louisiana

The Wedell-Williams Memorial Aviation Foundation, Members of the Board, Patterson, La.